Praise for

The Plantiful Table

"With inspiring flavors from Japan to Latin America, these recipes will definitely entertain the palate. Whether you're looking for vegan meal ideas or simply looking to cook more wholesomely for the family, this cookbook is a delight."

—ALI MAFFUCCI, food blogger and *New York Times*–bestselling author of *Inspiralized*

"*The Plantiful Table* is a beautifully crafted book filled with approachable meal ideas for vegan and vegetable-loving families. Andrea is a modern-day earth mama and her voice is warm and welcoming. Picking up this book makes you feel as though you're at her family table."

—JESSICA NADEL, author of *Greens 24/7* and *Superfoods 24/7* and creator of the blog *Cupcakes and Kale*

"With fun and inventive recipes like Hearts of Palm Patties and Indian Mango Pizza, Andrea Duclos shows us that plant-based eating can be something the whole family can get on board with (including the dog!). *The Plantiful Table* is a must for those looking to bring their family together to share healthy, hearty plant-based meals!"

—KRISTY TURNER, author of *But I Could Never Go Vegan!*

"*The Plantiful Table* is a fantastic book to get the entire family excited about healthy eating and dipping your toe into more whole-food recipes. Drea's love for being a mother and mother earth shines through each recipe!"

—MCKEL HILL, MS, RD, LDN, dietitian, nutritionist and creator of the blog *Nutrition Stripped*

THE EXPERIMENT

BECAUSE EVERY BOOK IS A TEST OF NEW IDEAS

The Plantiful Table

Easy, From-the-Earth Recipes
for the Whole Family

ANDREA DUCLOS

a cookbook from

ohdeardrea

THE EXPERIMENT
NEW YORK

The Experiment, LLC
220 East 23rd Street, Suite 301
New York, NY 10010-4674
www.theexperimentpublishing.com

This book contains the opinions and ideas of its author. It is intended to provide helpful and informative material on the subjects addressed in the book. It is sold with the understanding that the author and publisher are not engaged in rendering medical, health, or any other kind of personal professional services in the book. The author and publisher specifically disclaim all responsibility for any liability, loss, or risk—personal or otherwise—that is incurred as a consequence, directly or indirectly, of the use and application of any of the contents of this book.

The Experiment's books are available at special discounts when purchased in bulk for premiums and sales promotions as well as for fund-raising or educational use. For details, contact us at info@theexperimentpublishing.com.

Duclos, Andrea.
   The plantiful table : easy, from-the-earth recipes for the whole family / Andrea Duclos.
      pages cm
   Includes index.
   ISBN 978-1-61519-247-2 (cloth) -- ISBN 978-1-61519-248-9 (ebook)
1. Vegetarian cooking. I. Title.
   TX837.D77 2015
   641.5'636--dc23
                                    2015003784
   ISBN 978-1-61519-247-2

   Ebook ISBN 978-1-61519-248-9

Cover and text design by Sarah Smith
Cover photograph by Hannah Mayo
Author photograph by Hannah Mayo

Manufactured in China
Distributed by Workman Publishing Company, Inc.
Distributed simultaneously in Canada by Thomas Allen & Son Ltd.

First printing October 2015

10 9 8 7 6 5 4 3 2 1

To my parents, for believing in my potential.

To my daughter, for making me a better person.

And to my husband, for loving me for who I am.

I love you.

contents

introduction

The Story of an Ex French-frytarian

Welcome to my cookbook! I'm Andrea, but most people know me as Drea. I'm a lover of fresh air, hot sun, cool breezes, lush greenery, and plants. Lots of plants. Mostly eating them.

I didn't always feel this way. In fact, when I was growing up I hated vegetables—unless you count potatoes or corn, in which case, I loved vegetables. Okay, yes, I know that potatoes and corn are, technically, vegetables, but I tend to think of them more in terms of a starch and a grain, respectively, especially the way most people eat them these days. Either way, I'm pretty sure I didn't eat my full daily portion of healthy veggies as a kid. In fact, I don't think I tried salad until college, and even then, it was coated in ranch dressing. Other than the broccoli my mother sometimes forced upon me, I don't think I ate anything green. Thankfully, change is a constant part of life, and I eventually learned, at my own slow pace, that there was a delicious world beyond French fries at every meal, pasta smothered with cheese, and pizza nine times a week.

Gradually, I opened my taste buds to more options. I tried and retried mushrooms, broccoli, and tomatoes. I know, I know—an adult who's scared of tomatoes! Let me be honest: Even to this day I only like tomatoes when they're cooked. If I'm going to have a raw tomato, it needs to be (or I would prefer it to be) a fresh heirloom variety. At the very least a perfectly ripe organic tomato. Does this mean I'm still picky? Maybe—but I consider it craving only the highest quality in taste. I've been told that picky eaters make the best cooks, and I like to believe it.

These days, there isn't a fruit or vegetable I won't eat or at least try—well, except bananas (see page 60 for more on that little quirk and how I get around it). Is this transformation a miracle or an earth-shattering story? No, but it is a good life lesson that, whether you're a child or an adult, even taking little steps, one day at a time, can open up a world of possibilities.

Here I am now—happy, healthy, and thriving, with a small but oh-so-wonderful family that loves eating plants and plant-based foods as much as I do. To be honest, there's a chance that, if offered the opportunity, I'd still eat pizza nine times a week and French fries with every single meal, but these days, my (that is, our) meals consist mostly of vegetables and other whole foods, with little bits of indulgent pleasures here and there. You'll see for yourself, in the recipe section starting on page 23, that it's a delightful balance of good-for-you and tastes-so-good. Just because I've embraced a diet of mostly plants, that doesn't mean I'm a stranger to life's more indulgent, fried, gluttonous pleasures.

Besides being a tomato critic, pizza lover, and ex French-frytarian, who am I? Well, I'm a blogger. (If you just cringed a bit, I confess that I do the same every time I say the word "blogger"—but, well, that's what I am and what I love to do.) It's actually pretty awesome. I've been at it for about five years, and as I've grown and changed, so has my blog, *ohdeardrea*. It's amazing to spend my time connecting with people across the world who hold so many of the same loves, values, and yearnings to grow. I would blog for that reason alone.

As I've shared my ever-growing appreciation for natural foods and, more important, my interest in helping families eat healthfully, my readers have helped me discover that, although I may not have a culinary school degree, you don't need to be a professional chef to create delicious, wholesome recipes that everyone will love. Through my blog, I hope to inspire people to cook more real, whole-food meals for their kids—adventurous eaters and picky feeders alike. If I make just a small difference in how a family eats, I know that it can blossom into much bigger, even happier changes.

I want to show potential cooks that preparing healthy food is not about knowing every last technique or about being classically trained; it's about wanting to do it and then taking the necessary steps. Even one step forward is progress!

What's day-to-day life like in the *ohdeardrea* home and kitchen? For starters, I'm lucky enough to live in a bright, cheery house in South Florida with my beautiful family. My family consists of my husband, Alex, a talented chef and gifted bread-maker (you'll see some of his contributions throughout the recipe section), and my toddler-kiddo-daughter, Marlowe, who makes delicious kale pesto, guacamole, and, thanks to my mother, now knows the proper measurements to make rice (but as Marlowe will tell you, "I'm not allowed to use the stove").

Marlowe is a vegan like myself—or vegan-ish, depending on how strictly you view the rules. We do eat honey, but nothing else from the animal world. You can, however, find dairy milk and cheese in our home, because, well . . . Alex. He's not vegan or vegetarian or anywhere near those things. Are meals difficult for us as a mixed-food family? Not at all. With the exception of the late-night eggs that Alex sometimes fries up or his fresh mozzarella on pizza days, we don't make separate

meals. I think we're a pretty good example that meals don't have to be labeled as "vegan" or "not vegan"—it's all just food.

Our house is sweet, and we enjoy living in Florida. We're always working on ways to improve our home and garden, and we try to spend our spare time outdoors, venturing to farms or botanical gardens as much as possible. I love the changing and learning that takes place as I grow with my family. I love the care we put into our food and our rarely rushed meals. In the summer we sometimes feel trapped inside from the heat, but in the warm winters we thrive. No matter the season, though, our life revolves around our vibrant space and the food we raise, buy, make, and eat in it.

My life hasn't always revolved around food, but food has always been a large part of my life, just as it is for so many of us. With each passing year, the importance and love of eating well grows in me. Beginning with my personal experiences, and then having a child of my own, I've come to see how very important it is to pass down the knowledge and the reality that eating good food is vital, that it's one of the most important relationships in our lives—especially for our health and well-being. For this reason, we center our days around our food, our kitchen, and our table. We do it for ourselves and for one another.

Food doesn't have to be extravagant or complex to please people, and you don't need to put in a ton of time and work to create nourishing food. I firmly believe that with just a few fresh vegetables and richly flavored spices, you can create a truly amazing meal. What I do isn't about a desire to be a world-recognized cook or "celebrity chef"—I don't want or need any of that, nor do I think I would qualify for such titles. What I do want, wholeheartedly, is to keep living this simple, healthy life with my family, where we take the time to grow our own food and spend a little part of each day preparing a meal full of love.

I hope that I can share a bit of what I know and love with anyone who cares to read my words. Good food makes you feel good, inside and out. What you eat affects your mind, your body, and your heart. I want to show that eating good food—with ingredients straight from the earth—doesn't have to be difficult. Real food is attainable and affordable. Whether your family is one person or eight people, healthy, comforting meals packed with vegetables and nutrients can very easily be a part of a happy home, every day.

The Idea: Unprocessed, Vegan, Plant-Based Foods

This cookbook is here to help you create really, really delicious and healthy plant-based dishes, whether you grew up eating salads at every meal or devouring French fries as a meal. Although I'm certain everyone could live off vegetables alone (and enjoy it!), my goal isn't to convince people of that—if you decide to scramble an egg with your meal, don't worry: You won't find any angry vegans here. My only aim is to inspire people to spend more time in the kitchen or in a garden, learning about food, caring about food, and cultivating a love for vegetables and other unprocessed foods along the way. Bonus points if you pass along the knowledge you gain to your friends or children!

In my perfect, ideal universe we would all subsist on plants alone and make everything completely by hand. However, the world doesn't work this way, and, honestly, neither does my home. We make a lot of our food from scratch (most things, in fact), but you'll notice that we do buy some pre-made goods, too, such as pasta, yogurt, or milk. Can you make these items yourself at home? Absolutely, and it's great to do as much of that as you can. But in a world where grocery stores consist of aisle upon aisle of processed, ready-to-eat products, choosing only a small handful of simple pre-made items, rather than a whole cart of them, can still make a positive impact on your health and outlook.

I've tried my best to include as many quick, easy, handmade meals as possible within this book. Maybe you already make most of your meals from scratch—in which case, wonderful! If you don't, that's just fine, too—within these pages you'll find countless tasty, accessible, plant-based meals to bring new sparkle to your daily or weekly menu. I very much hope you find all the inspiration you need within these pages!

The Inspiration: Approachable, Family-Friendly, Everyday Recipes

With this book, I wanted to create something approachable, helpful, and fun, all while sharing my favorite foods. I tried to include a little bit of everything in here, from comfort food to family-focused dishes to easy snacks and meals. My goal was to provide recipes that truly satisfy adults and that are easy to adapt for young, developing taste buds. Some of the recipes take extra prep time or are intended to impress, but most were created to be filling and quick to make, while still soothing your heart and nourishing your body.

There aren't any magic vegan spells in here, and I'm not going to tell you to use portobello mushrooms as hamburger buns. While I do frequently use beans in many traditionally meaty dishes, in no way do I expect you to pretend that beans are meat—they're not, though they are wonderful in and of themselves.

You may have seen variations of some of these recipes before, and maybe you even grew up with them. I've altered them to fit our household needs, whether that means minimizing cooking time, removing dairy, adding in vegetables, erasing the need for meat, or just doing a general overhaul to create something that's more family-friendly and more "us." We're a family that cares about healthy food, but, more important, we're a family that loves food that tastes good.

You'll see some traditional American meals in this book, although not too many—I wanted to include a nice mix of flavors from all over the world, since our family meals are inspired by many cultures and cooking styles. With my mother's side of the family coming from Colombia and Alex's coming from Cuba, we're especially no strangers to Latin American cooking and flavors. From our liberal use of cumin and smoked paprika to plantains and beans, there's no denying the influence our parents have had on us. Some of the recipe sections have even been broken up by flavor and style of food—such as Latin American Favorites (page 159) or Asian Curries, Noodles, & Rices (page 189)—in celebration of the many different ingredients and cultures that inspire our daily meals.

Growing up, my mother made two separate meals every single night: One for the adults and one for the kids (my younger brother and myself). She believed, correctly, that there was no way we would eat the food she made for herself. At nine and ten years old, not even bribery could have convinced us to eat a meal that was so eloquently translated from Spanish into English as "sweaty chicken." Was it impossible to make us eat? No, but it was a true challenge.

Our mother, loving us dearly, busted her butt every evening to get us fed. We weren't malnourished, and we never starved, but my brother and I weren't exactly the most well-rounded or healthy kids in terms of eating. It was a struggle for all parties involved. While we all survived, I'm pretty certain (okay, completely certain) that it doesn't have to be that difficult. Nutritious food became incredibly important to me as soon as I found out I was pregnant, and I wanted to instill that importance in my daughter from the moment she was born. I knew if I wanted a healthy, thriving child, good nutrition would have to be a top priority.

Even though each child is different, I'm a good example of a picky, impossible-to-please kid who was able to grow up and help her daughter become the complete opposite. I didn't want to repeat the challenges my mother had faced, and I didn't want my daughter to deal with the food struggles I had suffered. If I can, I want to help others overcome these issues, too, even if just a little bit—and so I documented, photographed, wrote, and created this book in the hope that I can inspire others. Sure, I want to share recipes with hungry people, but I do it with a dream of helping families and kids everywhere become better eaters and love real food even more. Bye-bye, French-frytarians!

tips & tricks

You've probably noticed that this is a plant-based cookbook. (I mean, I hope you've noticed by now—I've mentioned it a few times!) Maybe you already live a plant-based lifestyle—hooray! If you're not a vegan but have this book in your hands, anyway—awesome! This is a fantastic, everyday cookbook for each and every one of you, especially since these recipes were created to be adaptable to you and your family's special needs and wants.

In this section, I'll guide you through some ideas for different ways to make the dishes work for you and anyone you feed. You don't have to be vegan to love this book—you just have to love food. Huzzah! It's a win-win all around.

For Eating Healthfully

These dishes were created to be easy and straightforward—I want you to open this book to a new recipe and proclaim, "Oooooh, I can do this!" (or, if playing it cool, a simple "I got this" works). So, you got this, right? This book will not (or at least should not) make you want to throw serving-ware across the room. It will help you create really tasty, filling, and (mostly) healthy meals to feed yourself and/or your family. Here are some of my favorite tips and tricks for creating flavorful dishes and having fun in the kitchen while doing so:

Relax, Drink Some Wine

Most people tend to unwind after a few sips of wine. Of course, you can relax in many different ways, perhaps by taking off your pants or blasting some good dance tunes, telling or listening to jokes, or cooking with a friend (doing all those things at once could be interesting, too). Whatever it is that helps take the stress off while you're cooking, do it—that's my advice.

While I fully understand the world of the serious, focused chef, I do believe that the best meals are made in happiness, and whether you're wearing pants or not, well . . . that's completely optional. So relax, make your cooking surroundings as enjoyable as you can, and go for it with your whole heart.

Know Any Good Salt Jokes? Na!

All right, so, without this becoming a lesson or a lecture (although I hope you enjoyed my bad chemistry joke above), I think we can agree that too much salt isn't great for you. But we can also agree that salt often makes things delicious! Seasoning your food is important. Spices, herbs, and salt can make or break a meal. Keep in mind that everyone's sodium tolerances, wants, and needs are different. For example, my husband is a salt fiend, and my mother avoids the stuff, while I can never agree with either of them on the proper salt level. I've decided that I fall somewhere in the middle, and the salt measurements are obviously my own personal recommendations—going through the book, it seems that the standard is around 1 teaspoon per recipe, where applicable— so please remember to taste your food as you go and determine whether your taste buds require more or less.

You'll find that many of the recipes call for you to add different ingredients at various times while cooking; my recommendation is to add a pinch of salt with each new addition. Example: Your onions and celery have cooked until translucent? Great, now add a sprinkle of salt before adding the next set of ingredients. The zucchini you added is cooked through? Sprinkle in another pinch before tossing in the tomato, and so on. If you're worried about over-salting, just make sure to taste-test frequently, and you should be fine. Pre-measure the amount of salt you'll ultimately use and place it in a small bowl next to your pot or pan, and—voilà—you can salt without worry as you go!

One final note about salting recipes: When you're making sauces intended to coat noodles or starchy vegetables, keep in mind that your sauce may need to be on the saltier (and more acidic) side. Once you sauce your noodles or veggies, the salt and acid will mix together to counter the starch, making your dish taste "just right."

Quality Control

To have the best-tasting meals, you need to start with the best-tasting (freshest) ingredients. Juice from a freshly squeezed lemon will taste a lot better than juice that comes out of your two-month-old, lemon-shaped plastic container. Spices will definitely add flavor to any dish, but using high-quality fresh spices will make your meal that much better.

SPICES, OILS, AND VINEGARS: The spice aisle of a market can be a somewhat scary place when you're first learning to cook. There are rows and rows of options, and each option comes in a different form—whole, ground, blended, and on and on forever. This is true for the oil and vinegar section, too. I've included a list of our favorite everyday spices, oils, and vinegars on page 20 in the Fridge and Pantry Staples section, which I hope will make the selection process a lot easier. Whether you decide to buy all the items on the list or just a few, remember that the best meals are made with the best ingredients, and the quality of your flavor-boosters makes a huge difference in the final product. Look at these ingredients as investments for your kitchen. We find the choicest spices at our local markets, and they're not that much more expensive (if at all) than our supermarket-purchased ones.

ORGANIC PRODUCE (ESPECIALLY HEIRLOOM TOMATOES): This should go without saying, but just as with spices and other ingredients, the quality of your fruits and vegetables matters. Not only is organic food chemical-free and GMO-free, you'll find that it's grown with more love and care, too, since these farmers have to invest extra time and labor in their crops. And, yes, love and care matter in plants (if you keep plants in your home, it's easy to see that). Think about it: Do you want a fruit that has been modified, sprayed, or injected with chemicals, or do you want something that was tenderly watched over and cared for and that's pesticide-free?

Thousands of resources these days provide tips on eating organically on a budget (including my blog, *ohdeardrea*, where you can find a basic pantry list, including costs, under "An Organic Shopping List and Vegan Pantry"). If you buy locally and seasonally, avoid processed foods, cook intelligently, and really utilize your leftovers, you shouldn't notice a big price jump in your weekly expenses. It may take a bit of readjusting and reprogramming of your brain and, more important, of your shopping list to make the change, but it's worth it.

If the chemicals used in and on many ingredients don't really bother you, that's fine, but do remember that flavor is important, too. I promise that your food will taste better if you switch to organic. I recommend buying one standard tomato and one organic tomato (both perfectly ripe, of course) and doing a taste-test. Which one tastes better? Which one is more watery? Which one is sweeter? Try it with watermelon, bananas, anything and everything. Compare and choose for yourself. Not only is organic produce naturally packed with flavor, it's also more nutritionally dense. It's a delicious win all around.

HERBS: As with the above items, quality herbs are important. Most of these recipes call for fresh herbs. We do stock some dried varieties in our pantry, but adding fresh ones to dishes adds a lot of flavor. But they can be expensive, right? And they go bad so quickly! I agree—fresh herbs can be tricky, so you have to make sure to buy them when you're absolutely positive you're going to use them. You'll see many of the same ones used repeatedly in my recipes, so it shouldn't be too hard to use up the whole bundle.

The best solution, though? Grow them yourself. Whether or not you plan to invest time in growing vegetables or fruit, herbs make easy and wonderful indoor or outdoor plants. They add life to your home and taste to your food, while also bringing down grocery expenses. A few well-chosen herbs (basil, oregano, and thyme should do the trick) can hold a lot of flavor-power, so you don't need a whole jungle in your house—just one windowsill with a few potted plants, and you should be good to go! I'd also like to emphasize that fresh herbs are not only delicious, they're also really, really good for you.

SEASONAL AND LOCAL: Another way to ensure that you're using the best-quality, most flavorful ingredients in your dishes is to buy your produce in season. Ideally, we would eat fruits and vegetables only when they're in season; unfortunately, that's not completely realistic or practical for feeding an entire family. Still, a fruit grown in season that's only traveled from a town or two over is probably going to taste a better than fruit that's been transported across the globe to get to the store, right? My motto for this (and everything, really) is "do what you can, when you can." It can help cut down on costs, too, so it doesn't hurt to give it a try!

Follow Your Heart and Your Gut

One of the most important things in cooking is to know what you like, love, and want to eat and to adjust your meals as necessary. I think that most—although not all—recipes should be looked at as a guide, which can help ease tension in the kitchen, too. This isn't to say that you should follow half the recipe and then wonder why the food didn't turn out the way it was supposed to; it doesn't work that way. But if the recipe calls for cilantro, and you loathe cilantro, then consider not using it or using less of it, or maybe substituting it with a similar ingredient that you don't hate. Meals are going to taste best not only with the choicest ingredients, but when they're made with the foods you love. So don't be afraid to follow your cooking instincts. Play, have fun, and just enjoy it.

Watch Some Food Movies (or Read Some Books*)

Movies revolving around food, from *Chocolat* to *Julie & Julia* to *Ratatouille*, can be good for the soul and can inspire people to get into the kitchen and cook. More important, though, I'm a big believer in food documentaries (see page 302 for a list of my top choices). Whether it's a movie about cooking, growing, farming, or whatever else, the more you know and the more you learn, the more you'll care. I hope so, anyway. It's really helpful to know where your food comes from, so if you're going to watch something, why not make it a food documentary? It may surprise you how entertaining they can be.

* I recommend movies over books only because it's easier to get the whole family actively involved, but books are obviously a great resource, too!

For Feeding Kids

I want to be clear that this isn't a "cooking for kids" book. Why? Because I don't think kids need to have separate meals than adults. I'm not an expert, and I'm not going to pretend to be, but I can share advice and guidance based on my own experiences and knowledge. My biggest tip for getting children to eat vegetables and enjoy all sorts of healthy foods is to start them on that path at a young age.

For example, because refined sugar has never been a part of my daughter's regular diet, she would simply never choose cake over a meal. Sure, she gets natural sugars from fruits and other whole foods, and we're not an entirely sugar-free family. Do I wish we were? Sometimes. Am I anti-sugar? No—sometimes you want and deserve a cookie, and there is simply no replacement for that. But I do make it a point to remember, for kids and adults both: Everything in moderation. A good kid-friendly snack is a piece of fruit or an avocado sandwich. A special treat is a smoothie. A really, really special treat is a cookie, ice cream, or some chips. It doesn't necessarily have to be earned; it can be an occasional "just because" present.

Like any child, your kids are not going to want to eat what they're not familiar with and don't know. This is a great thing to keep in mind when you a have a baby. Once you pass the stage of regularly introducing new foods and are well into the toddler or grade-school years, varying your child's diet can get a bit tricky, but it is absolutely still possible to make a change. Reasoning doesn't always work with kids, so you're probably out of luck trying that route (sorry—but there are still ways to encourage healthy eating, which I'll cover in a moment).

The more junk you eat, the more junk you crave. While this has been scientifically proven, it doesn't take a scientist to know that we all operate this way. But there is always a way to make a positive change—it just takes some time, effort, and patience. Like many things in life, these are improvements worth making, even if the progress is slow. To help you down the path, I've put together some of my best-loved tips and tricks for you and your family. Some of them are specific to babies, some are for toddlers, and some will work for any age.

Textures and Shapes

I refer to us as "texture people"—those who can't get past certain textures in food in order to enjoy it. If you're not a texture person (or have no idea what I'm talking about), count yourself lucky. We're not crazy, though: Textures play an important part in a human's desire to eat certain foods. No matter how wonderful mushrooms taste, it can be difficult to get past that chewy mouthfeel that mushrooms sometimes have.

It's good to keep this in mind when you cook for your children. Maybe your kids don't actually hate mushrooms; maybe they would just prefer them raw or roasted, diced up teeny-tiny or pureed. Make it a point to play around with different textures and shapes before giving up on an ingredient completely. Mushrooms are just one example, but there are a million and half ways to prepare any vegetable or fruit. It might be frustrating, but don't give up! Think of it as free, hands-on, learn-as-you-go cooking lessons for yourself.

Combined, Not Separated

A lot of people may not agree with me on this one—combining foods—but it's something I absolutely stand by when it comes to feeding children and introducing them to healthy eating. Other than allergy concerns, I see no reason to divide your kids' meals into separate finger foods. Even when serving adults this way (say, as appetizers or a snack tray), what are those adult going to do? Eat their favorite items and pass on the others. Kids are going to do this, too. When that happens, there's a good chance that they'll fill up on their top choices first (most likely the fats and carbs) and then not be hungry for the vegetables or proteins.

If allergies aren't an issue, try to make whole, one-pot style meals for your kids. Whether it's a soup or a veggie-packed rice and beans dish, serve everything all together. To make things easier, I've even included a "one-pot meal" icon to show which recipes are perfect for this. Picking at food is for the birds. Worried your kids won't like it? They're not going to become better eaters or healthier children by only eating the carbs on a plate. Whether you start with this method right off the bat or are attempting to make a positive food change with an older child, your kid will learn to love eating this way.

Mince It, Mince It Real Good

Now that we've explored how having a one-bowl type of meal can work for feeding your kids healthier ingredients, let's talk about how to improve on this idea for those especially picky little ones. You'll see different directions within my recipes for how to chop your vegetables; these describe how I think the dish is best served. But when prepping for a dinner with small, fussy children, consider finely chopping, well, basically everything. Not beans or things of that nature, but all your vegetables and herbs.

While this method won't teach your kids about the distinct flavors of each vegetable, you can always work on that later, once they're a little older and care about food a bit more, or when they can at least understand what you're trying to teach them! This idea works for now because it creates a dish that's flavorful, but in which it's difficult for children to pick out the specific flavors and avoid their least-favorite vegetables.

Focus on Flavors, Not "Kid Food"

Feeding children unseasoned food is another standard method of getting them to eat that I don't really understand or agree with. Unless someone has a tremendously oversensitive palate, there's no reason for anyone to prefer bland food. I'm not telling you to start coating everything in chili powder, but do make sure to flavor your food! And just adding salt isn't the solution to a bland-food problem; salt should always be moderated for little bodies (and big ones, too!).

Ingredients such as herbs and spices (not the spicy-hot variety, though) are a great way to add flavors and depth to food. If you start when they're young and stick to it, there's a good chance your kids will continue down this path! Just as with adults, though, you can't expect all children to like every flavor (though you should expect them to like a healthy variety of them). Your kid might not be a fan of turmeric, but perhaps the sweetness of garam masala will be a winner. Don't be afraid to play around with the seasonings. Kids want flavor, too—you don't need to "dumb down" food for them! Have them explore new flavors with you, whether it's smelling spices at the market or tasting herbs in a garden. Maybe you'll all find a few winners!

Get the Kids Involved

Asking children to participate in the cooking process, even with something as simple as smelling spices or picking herbs, makes them feel essential, excited, and interested to learn more about the food they eat. Yes, cooking with your kids requires a bit more time, patience, and cleaning up than whipping together a meal by yourself, but in the long run it's worth it. Kids are more likely to want to taste the things they make, so even if they don't love the food, having them contribute encourages them to try new ingredients and also understand the work and love that goes into making a meal. Don't limit yourself to the kitchen—get them involved throughout the whole process, from visiting the farm or market, to picking their own herbs in the garden, to choosing the recipe to make. Children are curious explorers by nature, and they might just surprise you.

Teach Them About Food

When you talk to your kids about food and the process of growing it, harvesting it, and creating a meal, you're teaching them the importance of each dish you make and how truly incredible our food system is. If they simply walk up to a plate of food every day and don't understand how it got there, kids won't consider what they're eating, why they're eating it, and the many steps it took to get it from the farm to the table. They just eat it (or don't), and that's that.

Explain to your kids why certain foods are good for them, that food provides nutrients for their bodies and how that helps them grow. Tell them why sugar and bad fats don't add anything beneficial to their diet but can be enjoyed in moderation because it's good to have little pleasures—sometimes. Teach them about how the food they eat is grown and how it's harvested, about how many people it involved and the time it took to get to their plate. Kids have questions. They like to know the "why." Don't just place a meal in front of them and expect them to realize its importance; teach them. They want to know.

Lead by Example

In addition to teaching your kids about food, it's important to lead by example. If you show your children bad eating habits, they'll likely retain some of those for themselves. You know why we sometimes have cookies in our house? Because I crave cookies. Not Marlowe—me. Introducing cookies was my own delicious fault! I'm still an absolute junk-food lover, but we try to keep it to the bare minimum and only bring it in as an occasional treat. Why? Well, because I have little to no self-control when it comes to chocolate, and because I want my child to grow up in a healthy home with healthy habits. I make it a point to try new foods often, to learn more about different fruits and vegetables, and to talk about why we buy organic produce, because I want my daughter to see how natural and easy it can be to live this way—in hopes that she'll always continue to do so.

Fat and Sugar Leads to More Fat and Sugar

As humans, we're programmed to love and crave fatty and sugary foods, which would be fine if junk food wasn't so readily available. Mangoes (so much sugar!) and avocados (so much fat!) are awesome natural foods to crave, but when you bring things such as cookies and French fries into the picture, our taste buds basically call everything else almost boring. Note that I said "almost boring," not "boring"—mangoes and avocados are never truly boring.

Wouldn't it be wonderful if we were programmed to crave only salads? That may not be the case, but we can certainly train our taste buds to fall in love with healthy foods, to want them more often, and to reduce our habitual desire for salty, sugary foods. The truth is, the more healthy food you eat, the more healthy food your body will want. Try it yourself. Give yourself two to three weeks without any sugar, and see if your body craves it after the two-week point. Sure, it's not easy changing someone's diet, especially a kid's, but after a certain point in time, the cravings stop, and eating healthily becomes easier—your body doesn't even really want the bad stuff anymore.

Start Early in the Day

Starting early in life is the best path to healthy eating, but no matter the age of your children, one of my better tips for winning the battle is to start early in the day. Chances are you're a pretty busy person with a hectic schedule. And chances are you're pretty pooped at the end of the day, right? Let's assume your kid is, too. So when the evening hits and mealtime rolls around and everyone involved is tired, how easy will it be to convince your kid to eat vegetables? How will your patience hold up? Trying to convince your kid to step away from the junk and toward the healthy food can be tough at any point, but it's definitely hardest at the end of a long day.

If you're home with your kids during the day, make lunch the healthy-meal goal. Schedule your lunchtime, and don't rush it. Make that a priority, and stick with it. Come nighttime, you'll feel much less guilty about giving in to fewer vegetables and more starch. It might feel a bit backward to have larger, healthier meals at lunch and easier, more carefree dinners in the evening, but, man, will it save you many tired, cranky, late-in-the-day battles! If you have school-age children or work daytime hours away, plan early dinners. And, again, schedule it. Yes, you're tired; yes, you want the kids to go to bed; yes, you probably still have a mile-long list of things to do; but if you can, start your dinners earlier, not when you're all half asleep.

For Leftovers

Leftovers seem to fall into the category of something you either love or hate, with not much in-between. The important thing to keep in mind, even if you dislike the idea, is that leftovers don't have to be boring repeats of the same dish—there are a lot of different delicious meals you can create using leftovers. They're a big part of my family's routine, and my life depended on them when I was taking care of a (constantly) nursing baby.

While I wouldn't try to impress a group of guests with leftovers—unless maybe you're throwing a leftover-themed party*—they're a great way for you to waste less food, save more time, and spend less money. Almost every recipe in this book contains a leftover tip (or two). Each piece of advice I offer is something that we commonly do at home with our own leftovers. Don't let your imagination stop with my suggestions, though; the possibilities are endless. I've rounded up some of our favorite go-to ideas here to get you started.

CALENTADO: Calentado, which you'll find on page 48, is the ultimate leftovers meal. You can add so many different things to the recipe. Although it's traditionally a Colombian dish, why not have some fun and add in leftover Indian food if you're in the mood? Experiment with anything you want!

QUESADILLAS/BURRITOS: If we don't create a rice-and-bean dish using our leftover beans, then I usually puree them as a quesadilla filling for Marlowe and myself. We both love this, and it works great with either of the bean dishes in this book (Black Beans, page 176, and Chili-Braised Pinto Beans, page 165). Cheese is a great addition to a quesadilla, but with smooth and creamy pureed beans, it's not necessary. Really, you can throw anything you love into a tortilla—leftover rice, potatoes, curries (just not all at once . . . okay, maybe all at once)—to make a quick and yummy quesadilla or burrito.

RICE & BEANS/FRIED RICE: Leftover beans or veggies can create easy, tasty dishes by just being mixed with rice, and leftover rice provides the perfect start to fried rice. Simply heat up your skillet, coat it lightly with olive oil, and gently pan-fry the rice and some fresh veggies, seasoning with herbs and spices as necessary.

SALAD TOPPINGS/WRAP ADD-INS: Sometimes I've shredded or chopped too many veggies when prepping to cook. Instead of tossing them out, I put them away until later that day or the next day to add to a salad or wrap. (If you want, you can try adding extras to dog food, too! Just remember, no onions for the pups—see page 294 for a list of the foods your canine friends should avoid.)

SOUP: Turn your old sauces into soup bases. This works especially well with red sauces or pesto. I use leftover red sauce as a base for many of our soup dishes. You can also use leftover potatoes as a base and thickener for creamy soups. On the other side of things, you can turn old soups into sauces. This is a great option for your more broth-heavy soups—just throw them back onto the stove, simmer, reduce, enhance, and—boom! Sauce for your pasta or veggies.

*Okay, I was half joking, but now that I've mentioned it, how fun would it be to throw a leftovers party? Invite all your friends over for a meal, send them home with the leftovers, and have them bring them back the next day for dinner party round two!

in our kitchen

Basic Tools for New Cooks

Before we head into the recipe portion of the book, I want to do a quick run-through of my family's favorite kitchen tools and gadgets. Most of my dishes are pretty straightforward and require very little in terms of tools or appliances. Some might call for a blender or food processor, but nothing that will break the bank. I tried not to include recipes that require fancy $400 blenders, dehydrators, ice cream makers, etc. So, with the exception of maybe the dough mixer, you should already have many of the items in your kitchen. If not, almost all the pieces here cost under $50 and should last you for years. For example, I've had a $30 immersion blender for six-plus years now, with a smoothie and soup count that is through the roof. It may not run as well as it once did, but it still does the job, many years and hundreds of meals later.

BAKING SHEET: If you don't already own this, you should buy one. They're pretty cheap. We use ours often, from making cookies to roasting vegetables, and you probably will, too.

BLENDER (STANDING OR IMMERSION): Some people prefer countertop blenders; others prefer the handheld immersion variety. Personally, I prefer an immersion blender, because it saves me the trouble of having to transfer hot, messy soup; plus, it's a smaller tool to clean up. A standard immersion blender will cost you around $30 and can be used for soups, smoothies, dressings, sauces, etc.

FOOD PROCESSOR: Food processors come in all sizes and prices. We managed with our small 2½-cup processor for years and years until we finally (just this year) upgraded to a larger 4-cup one. If you have a big family, splurge on a bigger processor. If it's just you, the little guy should do the trick!

GRATER: We have a ridiculously old, four-sided, tower-looking cheese grater in our house that works great for shredding carrots and beets. It's not an absolute necessity, but it definitely comes in handy.

HEAVY-BOTTOMED DUTCH OVEN POT: You really only need to invest in one of these (or maybe two, depending on the size of the meals you make). Whether you spend $40 or $200 on a heavy-bottomed pot, that one pot will take you a long, long way. A Dutch oven allows you to take your meal from the stove directly into the oven without any trouble. It can also double as a casserole dish and makes it simple to transport full meals for easy reheating at potluck dinner parties. We have a few in our house, since Alex and I combined kitchen accessories, but one large soup pot and a smaller rice pot are great items to add to your home.

HIGH-QUALITY KNIVES: Consider these to be investment pieces. No, you don't have to buy a $400 Japanese knife to make your meals, but you should plan to spend between $75 and $150 for a nice two-piece knife set. All you really need is a good chef's knife (maybe 8 inches long or so) and a sharp paring knife. With these two knives you can accomplish just about anything. (A bread knife is also good addition to your set.) Using a sharp knife will cut down on your prep time and frustration. It will also aid in the quality of the meals you produce and increase safety when cooking. Hooray for ten fingers!

MEASURING CUPS AND SPOONS: While these are fairly common household items, I figured I should add them to the list, just in case. I do believe in winging a lot of things and going with your gut when cooking (see the "Follow Your Heart and Your Gut" tip on page 11), but certain ingredients do need to be measured, especially when baking. It will save a lot of time, trouble, and possibly even failed recipes if you use a measuring cup and spoons. You can buy inexpensive ones at your local grocery store; you'll want two sets: One for liquids and one for dry ingredients.

NICE CUTTING BOARD: Okay, this isn't a necessity—a cheap one will do the trick, too—but a good, sturdy, wooden cutting board feels better and looks nicer in your kitchen. I also feel more inspired to cook when I'm using well-made, high-quality things, but that might just be me.

MICROPLANE ZESTER: This is a "must-have" on my list. I use it to make ginger and garlic pastes and to zest lemons and oranges. I don't use it every day or even every week, but I'd be lost without it on the days I need it.

MORTAR AND PESTLE: We love our mortar and pestle. Marlowe uses it often; I use it sometimes. It's a great tool not only for guacamole and salsa, but for everything from grinding spices to pressing herbs to pulverizing seeds. We own three of them. Yes, three. I know—it's a bit excessive. You really only need one. I would buy a small or medium set if you only intend to use it to grind things, and a larger set if you're interested in making salsa and guacamole for entertaining.

Fridge and Pantry Staples

You'll find many of the same ingredients mentioned throughout this book. These are our favorite go-to items that we usually keep on hand, since I think we can all agree it's pretty annoying to have to run to the store for a single ingredient that you only need for one recipe. And unless that ingredient has a long shelf life, chances are it's going to go bad before you use it up. To prevent this unnecessary wastefulness in our own lives (and your life, too!), we use the same staple ingredients repeatedly. Don't worry, though—you won't get stuck feeling as if you're eating the same food every day. Each dish has its own wonderful flavor and is very different from the next. With just a handful of high-quality fridge and pantry staples, the possibilities are endless.

So what's found in a mostly plant-based kitchen, you ask? A lot! Here you'll find a list of our most frequently used goods. Many are from our garden, many come from farmers' markets, and many, well, we just go to the store and buy—in season whenever possible! Words set in italics indicate an item used only occasionally but loved always. Additional information about ingredients marked with an asterisk (*) can be found in the Glossary on page 299.

FRESH VEGETABLES

Avocado	Mushrooms	Peppers
Artichoke	(white button or	(an assortment of
Cabbage (any color)	"baby bella"	spicy and sweet)
Carrots	mushrooms for	Potatoes (we keep white
Celery	everyday use; we buy	creamer potatoes)
Cherry tomatoes	the fancier varieties for	Radishes
Garlic	special occasions)	Tomatoes on the vine
Ginger	Onions	*Yuca*
Kale		

FROZEN VEGETABLES

Broccoli	Corn	Peas

FRESH FRUIT

Apples	Limes	Plantains
Bananas	Mangoes	Strawberries
Lemons	Oranges	

FROZEN FRUIT

Berries (any variety)

CANNED GOODS

Artichokes (we prefer
   fresh, but they're hard
   to find sometimes!)
Black beans

Chickpeas
Pinto beans

Tomatoes
   (crushed as well as
   peeled, whole ones)
White beans

DRIED GOODS

Israeli couscous
Lentils (red and green)
Quinoa

Rice
   (a few different types)

Pasta
   (a few different types)

FRESH HERBS

Basil
Cilantro

Dill
Mint

Oregano
Thyme

DRIED HERBS

Oregano

GROUND SPICES

Chili powder
Coriander
Cumin
Curry powder

Spicy smoked
Spanish paprika
(pimentón agridulce
*or picante)**

Sweet smoked
   Spanish paprika
   (pimentón dulce)*
Turmeric

WHOLE SPICES

Coriander
Cumin
Fennel

NUTS (RAW†)

Almonds

Cashews

Pine nuts

Pistachios

Walnuts

†We like to buy raw nuts, and roast or toast them as needed.

OILS AND VINEGARS

Coconut oil

Olive oil

Truffle oil

Vegetable oil (for
 occasional frying)

Apple cider vinegar

Balsamic vinegar

Red wine vinegar

Rice vinegar

Sherry vinegar

SPECIALTY/SOMEWHAT PROCESSED ITEMS ††

Almond milk (we buy
 whatever organic
 brand is on sale)

Coconut milk yogurt*
 (I recommend So
 Delicious Dairy-Free)

Dairy-free butter
 (we use Earth Balance,
 which you can find in
 tub or stick form at
 most grocers)

Egg replacer
 (Ener-G is our go-to)

Nutritional yeast*

Vegan cream cheese
 (such as Tofutti)

Vegan mayo
 (we prefer Vegenaise)

†† To be used sparingly

ICON KEY

 indicates one-pot dishes

 indicates Marlowe's favorite meals

breakfast
& brunch

easy tofu scramble

SERVES 4

wanted to start us off with one of the first recipes I ever posted on my blog. Not only because it's incredibly easy, but because it's a delightful breakfast—and we all know we should start the day off right. This dish has changed a bit since those early days, as I've replaced some of the packaged ingredients with more natural ones.

Tofu scramble makes a wonderful breakfast choice, since it's filled with vegetables and protein but isn't too heavy or nap-inducing. It's also perfect for the whole family, since you can easily add in or leave out items to adjust for individual tastes and preferences. Plus, you can use the leftovers in so many other dishes—see the Tip for Leftovers for some ideas!

1 tablespoon olive oil

1 small onion, small diced

1 cup (100 g) small diced mushrooms

One 14-ounce (about 400 g) package firm or extra-firm tofu, pressed and drained

2 garlic cloves, chopped

½ cup (90 g) chopped fresh tomatoes

1½ teaspoons nutritional yeast

½ teaspoon cumin

½ teaspoon salt

Black pepper to taste

Small handful of herbs, chopped (I recommend basil, parsley, and/or thyme)

Two handfuls of baby greens and/or spinach, chopped

1. Lightly coat the bottom of a medium pan with olive oil and place it over medium heat.

2. When the oil is hot, add the onion and mushrooms and cook until the onion is soft and translucent and the mushrooms are browned.

3. While the onion and mushrooms are cooking, crumble the tofu in a large bowl, then add all the remaining ingredients except the salt, pepper, herbs, and greens to the bowl. Mix well.

4. Add the tofu mixture to the pan and stir together with the onion and mushrooms. Cook until all the liquid is gone, then season with salt and pepper.

5. Mix in the greens and herbs, tossing until the greens are wilted.

6. Serve immediately. I like to make some toast to eat with this.

KID-FRIENDLY TIP: If you dice vegetables small enough and sauté everything together in one pan, it adds a bunch of flavor without making this an overly vegetable-y dish for picky eaters. So chop those veggies up and cook them thoroughly! The idea isn't necessarily to hide them, but to be able to incorporate them into your dish well and encourage your child's love of vegetables.

TIP FOR LEFTOVERS: Reheat anything that's left in a breakfast burrito or taco, or use it in Calentado (page 48) for a yummy brunch. You could even heat some up with rice and a splash of soy sauce for a quick and easy dinner.

tofu bhurji (indian scramble)

SERVES 4

absolutely adore savory foods for breakfast, and I love the rich flavors and spices of Indian food even more—I'd happily eat it for breakfast every day. Since reheating really spicy leftovers first thing in the morning gets a side-eye around my house, I decided to combine two of my favorite things into a delicious, family-approved breakfast. When you're craving an extra kick, just reach for this fun and sophisticated recipe—it's a great way to easily spice up your morning with a flavorful and super-healthy kick.

1 tablespoon olive oil or coconut oil

1 small onion, small diced

1 jalapeño, seeded and thinly sliced

1 cup (100 g) chopped cauliflower or creamer potato

One 14-ounce (about 400 g) package firm or extra-firm tofu, drained and pressed

½ teaspoon coriander

½ teaspoon cumin

½ teaspoon turmeric

½ teaspoon salt

1-inch (2.5 cm) piece of ginger, peeled and minced

2 garlic cloves, chopped

Salt and black pepper to taste

Small handful of cilantro, chopped

¼ cup (35 g) peas

1. Lightly coat the bottom of a medium pan with the oil and place it over medium heat.

2. When the oil is hot, add the onion, jalapeño, and cauliflower and cook until the onion is soft and translucent.

3. While the vegetables are cooking, crumble the tofu into a large bowl, then add the spices, along with the ginger and garlic. Mix well.

4. Add the tofu mixture to the pan with the vegetables and cook until the liquid is gone. Season with salt and pepper.

5. Mix in the cilantro and peas. Serve immediately, preferably with some pita triangles.

KID-FRIENDLY TIP: Skip the jalapeño and chop the cauliflower nice and small.

good
morning!

THE PLANTIFUL TABLE

arepas with hearty corn & avocado salsa

SERVES 3 TO 4 // MAKES 2 CUPS [ABOUT 275 G] SALSA

Just like toast (see page 51 for an entire section of Things on Toast!), the options for arepa toppings are limitless. Arepas can be a tad starchy and heavy, so I find that serving them with a refreshing salsa is a good middle ground between trying to convince yourself that this dish is healthy for you and knowing that it's just a deliciously satisfying meal—not junk food, not health food, just good, Latin American, morning comfort food.

1. In a medium bowl, combine the liquids, herbs, and garlic. Add the cherry tomatoes and gently mix.

2. Heat 1 tablespoon of the oil in a medium skillet or frying pan over medium-high heat.

3. Add the corn, along with a heavy sprinkling of salt and a crack of pepper. Allow it to fry until a slight char develops, about 5 minutes. Set aside to cool.

4. Add the avocado and the corn into the salsa mixture and gently mix.

5. Taste and adjust the seasoning as necessary, then layer over warm, freshly made arepas.

A NOTE ABOUT THIS RECIPE

I'll probably repeat this a million times over the course of this book, but I didn't grow up in what you might call a traditional American household, especially in a culinary sense. Sunday mornings we didn't have eggs, bacon, or toast—we had arepas.

3 tablespoons olive oil + 1 tablespoon for frying

1 tablespoon lime juice

2 tablespoons red wine vinegar or sherry vinegar

1 tablespoon water

2 tablespoons chopped cilantro

1 tablespoon minced chives

¼ teaspoon minced garlic

1 cup (150 g) quartered cherry tomatoes

1 cup (160 g) fresh or frozen corn

Salt and freshly cracked black pepper to taste

1 avocado, pitted, peeled, and diced

Arepas (page 183 or 184)

everyone's favorite breakfast potatoes

Without fail, every person who tries these potatoes falls in love with them. Before putting together this cookbook, though, I'd never had to put the recipe into exact words and numbers. As with most of our meals, we just wing it and slightly tweak the dish every time to fit our cravings and kitchen supply. Sometimes I'm the one throwing them together; sometimes it's Alex in front of the stove. I think the only real difference between our recipes is the amount of oil—he has a slightly heavier hand with it. All the spices, vegetables, and other additions are generally the same. We both love and expect a healthy helping of spice, along with crispy, colorful vegetables and fresh green herbs.

3 to 4 medium Yukon Gold potatoes, cubed

2 tablespoons olive oil

1 medium onion, sliced

½ red bell pepper, sliced

4 garlic cloves, sliced

2 teaspoons high-quality spicy smoked Spanish paprika

1½ teaspoons salt

Freshly cracked black pepper to taste

Fresh oregano and cilantro to taste

1. Blanch the potatoes in salted boiling water until slightly softened, about 5 minutes. Drain and set aside to cool.

2. Heat the olive oil in a heavy-bottomed sauté pan (preferably cast iron or black steel) over medium heat.

3. Add the onion, pepper, and garlic and cook until the onion is soft and translucent, about 10 minutes.

4. Mix the potatoes into the pan with the other vegetables. Continue cooking, tossing the potatoes continuously to allow each side to receive some color from the bottom of the pan.

5. After 5 minutes, add the paprika, salt, and pepper. Toss the mixture in the pan and cook until everything is a dark golden-brown.

6. At the very last second, toss in the fresh oregano and cilantro, then serve.

VARIATION:

Add some canned chickpeas (about 1 cup [164 g]) or a handful of kale. Those are our two favorite add-ins. Who doesn't like a bit of extra protein or calcium and fiber in their savory morning meal? If you want to use chickpeas, add them at the same time as the paprika. If you go with kale, mix it in before the potatoes. Toss until it's cooked down slightly, then add the potatoes.

KID-FRIENDLY TIP: Cut those veggies small and cook them until they're nice and soft, but make sure to leave the potatoes on the bigger side to keep them from overcooking into mush.

TIP FOR LEFTOVERS: These are an excellent addition to Calentado (page 48).

biscuits with mushroom gravy

SERVES 4 MAKES 2 TO 3 CUPS OF GRAVY

This is probably one of the least attractive meals I make, but it's also one of the most delicious. Marlowe begs for it like it's her job. And you know what? I don't mind putting it together for her. Even though the recipe involves both biscuit-baking and gravy-making, it's surprisingly easy—she could probably even make them herself (with a little help from me, of course). It's also an incredibly comforting dish and, hey, packed with nutritious mushrooms!

1 ⅓ tablespoons dairy-free butter

2 cups (200 g) small-diced mushrooms (choose your favorite variety—we typically use baby bellas, since that's what we have on hand, but any kind will work great)

1 cup (160 g) small diced onions

2 tablespoons flour

1 cup (250 ml) Vegetable Stock (page 116)

½ cup (125 ml) dairy-free milk

2 tablespoons chopped oregano and thyme

1 tablespoon nutritional yeast

½ teaspoon salt

Black pepper to taste

Biscuits, pre-baked (page 266)

1. Melt the butter in a medium saucepan over medium heat.

2. Add the mushrooms and onions and cook until the onions are translucent and most of the liquid from mushrooms has cooked out. You can tell it's happening because the mushrooms will get much smaller.

3. Add the flour to the pan and mix well to create a roux.* The mixture will stick to bottom of the pan—this is good, since it browns the flour a bit and creates more flavor.

4. Quickly add small amounts of the stock, about ¼ cup (60 ml) at a time, whisking continuously. Make sure to scrape up any bits of flour that are stuck to the bottom of the pan and mix everything together well. The sauce should start to thicken.

5. Whisk in the remaining stock and then the milk, stirring until fully incorporated.

6. Add the herbs, nutritional yeast, salt, and pepper.

7. Simmer until the gravy has thickened to your desired consistency.

8. Slice open your freshly baked biscuits and serve with a ladleful of gravy on top.

A roux is a common thickener, used as the base for many sauces.

KID-FRIENDLY TIP: If I'm feeling extra health-conscious, I'll add lentils to create a more rounded meal. Either simmer ¼ cup (25 g) of soaked lentils in with the gravy, or add pre-cooked lentils at the end. It messes with the texture a bit, so I wouldn't make it this way to impress other adults, but if your goal is to impress your toddler and feed her a meal with both vegetables and protein, this helps—a lot.

A NOTE ABOUT THIS RECIPE

I wish I had a love story to share with you about this biscuits and gravy recipe, like how I grew up eating it every Saturday, or how it's been a tradition of mine for years. I don't have anything like that—I grew up in a home where breakfasts were very far off from the all-American biscuits and gravy—but I can say that I make and eat this, with love for my kiddo, each and every time she asks for it. And I'll happily make it for her and with her forever.

garam masala pancakes

A quick disclaimer: Try this recipe before you automatically give it the side-eye just because I'm suggesting that you put garam masala in your pancakes. These are light and fluffy, savory and sweet, and overall delicious. They work well for everyone who wants to try something new, whether you have a strong sweet tooth or you love a savory breakfast, like me.

2 Flax Eggs (recipe follows)

2 cups (250 g) all-purpose flour

3 teaspoons baking powder

½ teaspoon salt

3 tablespoons sugar

1 tablespoon + 1 teaspoon garam masala

2 cups (500 ml) almond milk (unflavored or vanilla)

2 tablespoons vegetable oil or dairy-free butter, melted

1 teaspoon grated ginger

Zest from 1 orange

¼ teaspoon vanilla extract

Dairy-free butter or oil for the pan

1. Prepare the Flax Eggs in a small bowl and allow the mixture to sit and thicken while you prepare the other ingredients.

2. Combine the dry ingredients in a large bowl and combine well. Set aside.

3. In another large bowl, mix together the wet ingredients, then add the Flax Eggs and combine well.

4. Slowly add the wet ingredients to the dry ones, mixing gently until everything is well combined and smooth.

5. Place a large griddle or pan over medium heat and add a dollop of the butter or oil. Using a ladle, pour some of the batter onto the griddle to create a circle (or a heart, if your kid is as heart-obsessed as mine) and cook for a few minutes. Once the batter begins to bubble, carefully flip the pancake and cook the other side until golden brown. Repeat this step until all your batter is gone.

6. Serve with syrup and/or Orange-Infused Coconut Whipped Cream (page 281).

flax egg

1 tablespoon ground flaxseed

3 tablespoons warm or room temperature water

Slowly add the water to the ground flax and stir until it begins to feel gooey, about 1 to 2 minutes. Allow the mixture to rest on the counter or in the fridge until ready for use. Yield can be increased proportionally depending on your needs.

tropical waffles

MAKES 4 TO 6 WAFFLES

I don't typically have a sweet tooth for breakfast—but waffles? There's just something magical about them. I grew up eating all kinds: waffles smothered with syrup, or covered with whipped cream and strawberries, or, best of all, topped with ice cream. Realistically, I probably ate two a day at one point in my life. And if you let me, I'd eat an entire box of the frozen kind, no problem. My point is: waffles are amazing. Although I think a waffle on its own is an absolute treasure, there are days when I feel like jazzing them up a bit and giving them a new, sunnier, summer makeover. While I won't claim that this recipe is the healthiest, I will say that it's a lighter and slightly healthier option than traditional waffles. One last thing—topping this with Orange-Infused Coconut Whipped Cream (page 281), mango ice cream, or maybe even both? Always a good idea.

2 cups (250 g) all-purpose flour

½ teaspoon salt

1½ teaspoons baking powder

1½ tablespoons sugar

3 tablespoons dried shredded coconut + extra for garnish

2 tablespoons egg replacer

¾ cup (185 ml) coconut milk

½ cup (120 g) coconut milk yogurt

¼ cup (55 ml) coconut oil + extra for cooking the waffles

Tropical fruit for topping, to taste

Honey or maple syrup for topping, to taste

1. Mix the dry ingredients together in a medium bowl and set aside.

2. In a large bowl, combine the egg replacer with the coconut milk and mix very well, until all the powder has completely dissolved.

3. Add the yogurt and the oil to the coconut milk mixture and stir until combined.

4. Fold the dry ingredients into the wet ingredients and combine them well. This mixture will be thick, and that's okay.

5. Brush the hot waffle iron with some coconut oil and make your waffles.

6. Top with diced mango, dragon fruit, kiwi, or any of your other favorite tropical fruits, then sprinkle with shredded coconut and drizzle with honey or maple syrup. Yum!

TIP FOR LEFTOVERS: Wrap any leftover waffles in aluminum foil and freeze. They take only seconds to reheat: simply place them in a hot skillet or in a toaster oven until warmed through. Spend a few hours one weekend making a huge batch of them to store in your freezer. You'll never buy boxed waffles again!

sourdough french toast with roasted fruit

You might not believe it, but delicious French toast is 100 percent possible without eggs. All you need is some sourdough bread, almond milk, and roasted fruit, and you can create magic.

¾ cup (93 g) all-purpose flour

1½ cups (350 ml) vanilla almond milk

1 teaspoon vanilla extract

Pinch of salt, or to taste

Dairy-free butter or coconut oil for cooking

8 to 10 thick slices sourdough bread

Roasted Fruit to taste (recipe follows)

1. Pour the flour into a bowl wide enough to fit a slice of bread. Slowly add the milk to the flour, whisking vigorously.

2. When the flour is completely incorporated into the milk and no clumps are left, whisk in the vanilla extract and a tiny pinch of salt.

3. Melt a teaspoon of the butter or coconut oil in a skillet over medium heat.

4. Quickly dip a slice of bread into the batter, just long enough to coat it, and then place it on the hot, buttered skillet.

5. Cook the bread on each side for 1 to 3 minutes, until golden brown.

6. Once all the bread has been battered and cooked, place the French toast in a large serving dish, pour your Roasted Fruit on top, and serve.

TIP FOR LEFTOVERS: If you somehow don't finish this meal at breakfast, just leave it on the counter. Ten bucks says it'll be gone in a few hours.

Recipe continues...

yum!

roasted fruit

2 ripe peaches, sliced
1 ripe pear, sliced
1 cup (110 g) blueberries
2 tablespoons sugar

1. Preheat the oven to 450°F (230°C).

2. Combine the ingredients in a large bowl and toss to coat all the fruit evenly with the sugar.

3. Spread the fruit on a large baking sheet and roast for 15 minutes, until the peaches and pear have developed some color.

sticky buns

Full disclosure: this is my husband's recipe. When we first discussed making a "nutty breakfast bread," I had envisioned healthy, whole-grain goodness. But I left him to it, and when I looked up—*boom*! Gloppy, delicious, syrupy, sugary goodness had happened instead. This isn't the type of breakfast I normally choose, but from the moment you put these in front of me, I say, "Hmm, I don't think so," and then I eat six. Be warned—they're extremely addicting and very hard to say no to.

PRE-FERMENT

200 ml (⅞ cup) water

200 g (1½ cups + 1 tablespoon) all-purpose flour

⅛ teaspoon instant yeast

DOUGH

Pre-ferment

438 g (3⅓ cups + 2 tablespoons) all-purpose flour

5 tablespoons sugar

1 teaspoon salt

2 teaspoons instant yeast

Zest of 1 lemon

½ teaspoon vanilla extract

250 ml (1 cup) dairy-free milk

5 tablespoons dairy-free butter, softened

85 g cinnamon-sugar mix (6 tablespoons sugar + 2 tablespoons cinnamon)

CARAMEL GLAZE

170 g (¾ cup) dairy-free butter, softened

100 g (½ cup) lightly packed brown sugar

100 g (scant ½ cup) white sugar

½ teaspoon salt

1 teaspoon vanilla extract

130 g (about 1¼ cups) chopped nuts of your choice (we love almonds, pecans, and/or walnuts)

2 teaspoons flaxseeds

1. The night before you want to make the sticky buns, combine all the ingredients for the pre-ferment in a medium bowl and mix until just incorporated. Allow the mixture to sit on the counter, covered, overnight.

2. The next day, combine all the ingredients for the dough, except the butter and the cinnamon-sugar, in a stand mixer with a dough hook on low speed for 2 minutes, until fully incorporated. Let the dough rest for 15 minutes.

Recipe continues...

THE PLANTIFUL TABLE

3. Turn the mixer to medium speed and knead the dough for 8 to 10 minutes, until smooth and glossy. While the mixer is still going, slowly add the butter, 1 tablespoon at a time.

4. Once all the butter is added and the dough no longer sticks to the bowl, remove the hook and cover the bowl with a kitchen towel. Allow the dough to rise for about 2 hours, until doubled in size.

5. In the meantime, start the caramel glaze: in a large bowl, combine the butter, sugars, and salt, and beat until smooth and fluffy, by hand or with the mixer. Mix in the vanilla.

6. Spread the glaze across the bottom of a 9 x 13-inch (23 x 33 cm) baking pan. Sprinkle the nuts and seeds on top of the glaze and place the pan in the refrigerator to chill while the dough rises.

7. After the dough has doubled in size, move it to a floured work surface. Using a floured rolling pin, roll out the dough into a ½-inch (1.25 cm) thick rectangle.

8. Sprinkle the dough with the cinnamon-sugar mixture and roll it up lengthwise, like a log. Slice the log into twelve equal pieces. Place each piece cut side up in the baking dish and cover with a dish towel. Allow them to rise for another hour. They may or may not double in size again, but they will get larger.

9. Place the oven rack on the lowest setting and preheat the oven to 350°F (175°C). Bake the buns for 30 to 35 minutes, until they develop a rich, golden-brown hue.

10. Allow them to cool until you're able to handle them, then carefully place a large plate or tray on top and flip over. Remove the baking dish, pull apart, and eat!

NOTE: You will notice that I've listed metric measurements first, since I highly recommend using those to ensure the best possible results for your yeast dough.

chocolate chip scones

MAKES 8 TO 10 SCONES

I'm not sure who decided to put scones into a breakfast category. For me, this is a far stretch from breakfast—unless, of course, there's a special occasion that deserves a chocolate-, flour-, and sugar-filled breakfast. Nonetheless, scones for breakfast are very real and much loved, so I created this perfect vegan chocolate chip scone recipe that you see here.

1 to 1½ cups (250 to 350 ml) almond milk (or dairy-free milk of choice)

1 tablespoon apple cider vinegar

3 cups (375 g) self-rising flour

1 tablespoon baking powder

1 teaspoon baking soda

½ cup (113 g) sugar

8 tablespoons dairy-free butter or other vegan butter substitute

2 teaspoons vanilla extract

About three-quarters of a 12-ounce (280 g) bag of vegan dark chocolate chips, depending on how chocolatey you want your cookies to be

1. Preheat the oven to 400°F (200°C).

2. Combine the milk and vinegar in a medium bowl and set aside for about 5 minutes, allowing the mixture to curdle.

3. In a large bowl, combine the flour, baking powder, baking soda, and sugar. Mix well.

4. Separate the butter into chunks and place it into the bowl with the dry ingredients. Using your hands, combine the butter into the flour mixture. Break it up as much as you can, until all the butter is completely incorporated.

5. Mix the vanilla into the milk and vinegar mixture.

6. Slowly add the wet mixture to the bowl with the dry ingredients and combine them well. The dough will be wet and sticky, but it should be manageable. Once it's completely formed, mix in the chocolate chips.

7. Knead the dough on a floured surface for 2 minutes.

8. On a floured baking sheet or parchment paper, flatten the dough into a 1½-inch (4 cm) thick circle.

9. Slice the dough into triangles and bake for about 25 minutes, until the crust is golden and flaky and the scones are cooked through.

10. Allow them to cool, then rip apart and enjoy!

THE PLANTIFUL TABLE

sweet & smoky tempeh

This is as close as we get to mock meat around my house. I'm fully aware that tempeh is nothing like meat—it's not a mock meat product, and it will never convince a meat lover to forgo bacon. That said, this dish is a great addition to your list of sides for breakfast or brunch. The tempeh tastes incredible after marinating overnight, but if you're in a rush or decide to make this on a whim, marinating first is not a necessity. You can also use this in the Corn & Potato Chowder (page 128) or Split Pea Soup (page 120).

1. Bring a medium pot of water to boil. Place the block of tempeh (halved if necessary) in the pot and simmer for 5 to 8 minutes. Remove the tempeh from the pot and allow it to cool.

2. Slice the tempeh into thin strips, about ½-inch (1 cm) thick.

3. Combine all the other ingredients in a medium baking dish and place the tempeh in the mixture. Marinate for at least an hour, or overnight, if possible—either on the counter or in the fridge is fine.

4. When you're ready to cook the tempeh, place a skillet over medium-high heat and coat the bottom of the pan with oil.*

5. Add the tempeh to the skillet and cook, adding spoonfuls of the marinating liquid periodically and allowing it to caramelize the tempeh. Fry until golden brown.

6. Serve immediately. We like to pair this with just about any and all other breakfast items.

*You can bake the tempeh instead, if you want. Simply plop it on a baking sheet and into a 400°F (200°C) oven until all the liquid is dissolved—but you should know that it's more delicious cooked in a skillet.

One 8-ounce (about 230 g) package tempeh

2 tablespoons soy sauce

2 tablespoons maple syrup

1 teaspoon liquid smoke

1 teaspoon red wine vinegar

1 tablespoon olive oil + extra for frying

¼ cup (60 ml) water

calentado

Traditionally, *calentado* ("heated" in Spanish) is a Colombian dish created in the morning from the previous night's leftovers. In other words, my ideal meal. I love re-creating leftovers—and if I can eat them for breakfast, even better. Since all the ingredients in this recipe are common staple items in many homes, it's an easy morning meal. I typically make it after a taco dinner or with leftover scrambled tofu (such as the Easy Tofu Scramble on page 24), but if there are no leftovers to be found in your home, you can make it from scratch, and it will still be completely worth it.

1 tablespoon + 1 teaspoon oil, divided

1 small onion, diced

1 medium to large potato (any variety), medium diced

½ cup (80 g) fresh, frozen, or leftover corn

½ teaspoon salt, or to taste

2 garlic cloves, minced

½ teaspoon cumin

¼ teaspoon chili powder

½ teaspoon sweet smoked Spanish paprika

½ teaspoon dried oregano

1 cup (200 g) leftover tofu dish or Calentado Tofu Mixture (recipe follows)

½ cup (100 g) cooked long-grain rice

1 cup (170 g) pinto beans, rinsed and drained (or use leftover beans from taco night—those are best!)

1. Heat about 1 tablespoon of oil in a large skillet or frying pan over medium heat. Add the onion and cook until translucent.

2. Mix in the potato and place a lid on top. It doesn't need to be tight-fitting; you just want to cover the potato to allow it to steam a bit.

3. Cook for about 2 minutes and then remove the lid and gently toss the potato. You want to lightly fry the pieces on all sides, letting them cook through without burning. The trick to achieving this is to cut them into little pieces, about ½-inch (1.25 cm) cubes or smaller, and to lightly steam them first.

4. While the potato is frying, make the Calentado Tofu Mixture, if you're not using leftovers.

5. Add the corn and salt to the pan with the potato and fry for about 3 minutes.

6. Mix in the garlic and the remaining spices and herbs. Stir well and cook for another 1 to 2 minutes.

Recipe continues...

A NOTE ABOUT THIS RECIPE

At home my mother and grandmother would take all the leftovers from the previous night's dinner, reheat them (hence the recipe name) in a hot pan or skillet, and then add an egg, creating a hearty breakfast. As you might imagine, it included a decent amount of meat (usually chicken in our home). We never have meat leftovers at our house, but rice, beans, or rice with beans are not uncommon in our fridge, so I recreated the dish without the animal protein to fit our needs. No worries, though—if you love eggs and hate tofu, feel free to try it that way, too. You won't be dissatisfied either way.

7. Add the tofu mixture to the pan and cook until the liquid has almost completely evaporated.

8. Mix in the rice and 1 teaspoon of oil and fry until everything is heated through, about 5 to 8 minutes.

9. Toss in beans and cook for another minute or so, until heated through.

10. Serve with arepas (see page 182 or 184 for recipes), avocado slices, or simply enjoy as is!

KID-FRIENDLY TIP: My mom let me eat calentado with ketchup growing up. And sometimes, just for fun, I offer it to Marlowe this way (now that I'm an adult, I add hot sauce to mine). Honestly, if I thought of it, I would probably still eat it with ketchup to this day. In fact, I'm not really sure why I don't. See page 252 for my homemade Ketchup recipe if you want to give it a try.

calentado tofu mixture

MAKES 1 CUP (200 G)

Half of a 14-ounce (about 400 g) tofu
   package, drained and pressed

1 teaspoon salt

1½ teaspoons nutritional yeast

½ teaspoon annatto powder (optional)

Crumble the tofu into a medium bowl and add the salt, nutritional yeast, and annatto powder, if using. Mix together and then set aside until needed.

things
on toast

pea pesto

SERVES 4

This is a favorite at our breakfast and brunch table. Well, all toast is, but this version joins us at family feasts more than others. It brings a lightness, a touch of green, and a healthy scoop of veggies to any plate. Depending on Marlowe's mood, she either adores it or says "no, thank you," but she typically devours most of it. This is a great dish to bring to parties since it's easy to make and easy to enjoy.

½ cup (70 g) toasted whole almonds

1 cup (140 g) fresh English peas

1 garlic clove

Juice and zest of 1 lemon

1 teaspoon salt

Black pepper to taste

Handful of fresh parsley

Handful of fresh cilantro

6 tablespoons olive oil

1 tablespoon water

4 to 6 thick slices of sourdough bread, toasted

1. Combine all the ingredients—except the bread, of course—in a food processor and puree into a paste. A little texture is okay.

2. Schmear some pesto onto the toast and eat!

KID-FRIENDLY TIP: Omit one of the herbs or switch it out for a more kid-approved variety, such as basil.

TIP FOR LEFTOVERS: This pesto works beautifully just for snacking, too. It's great as a dip for raw veggies, as a spread for crackers, or in a wrap.

pear, radish & carrot (with radish tops)

SERVES 2

This recipe is simple enough that you can make it any (or every) day, but it's still interesting enough that you feel like you're eating something extraordinary—because it is. As far as "things on toast" goes, this is also considerably healthy since you've got fruit, vegetables, and even greens in there. Everything combines together perfectly, and it's so much more interesting than just a salad and bread.

1. Remove the radish tops and soak them in a bowl of water for at least 10 minutes.

2. While the radish tops soak, slice or julienne the radishes, pear, and carrot very thinly.

3. Clean your radish tops—they can be really dirty, so it's important to soak them for a while and to clean them thoroughly to avoid finding bits of soil on your toast. Roughly chop them if they're on the bigger side.

4. Heat the oil in a medium skillet over medium heat.

5. Add the carrot and sauté for a few minutes, until they begin to soften.

6. Mix in the pear and radishes, tops included, and sauté for another few minutes.

7. Drizzle the honey on top and sauté for a few more minutes, until the veggies are slightly brown.

8. Add the basil, if using.

9. Place the mixture on top of the toast. Add another drizzle of honey, sprinkle with salt, and enjoy!

1 bunch of radishes
(about 6 to 8), stems
attached and greens
removed*

1 pear

1 carrot

Olive oil for cooking

Honey or agave syrup to taste

Fresh basil to taste
(optional)

2 thick slices sourdough
bread, toasted

Salt to taste

Recipe continues...

an extra chop-chop-chop, and
maybe skip the radish tops.

What do you guys do with your radish tops? Soup? Juice? I imagine many people just throw them away—they do seem endlessly and impossibly dirty, right? But it doesn't have to be that way! Just soak them in a big bowl of water for about 10 minutes before washing and rinsing them twice, then use them in this recipe or any other recipe that calls for radishes. You'll never waste these nutritious, flavorful little pieces again.

VARIATION:

Try spreading this with some mashed avocado for a little bit of creaminess.

simply amazing tomatoes & roasted garlic

SERVES 4

The reality when making roasted garlic for toast is that 99.9 percent of the time it does not even make it to the bread. It pops out of the oven, onto a fork, and into the mouth. If you can somehow muster up enough self-control to create this dish in full, kudos to you. Overflowing with herbs, fancy oils, and heirloom tomatoes, it's a wonderful and easy recipe for entertaining. And since everyone will be eating it, you won't have to worry about your own garlic breath. It's a win all around!

1. Preheat the oven to 400°F (200°C).

2. Using a sharp, serrated knife, slice the top part of the garlic head off to expose the tops of the cloves.

3. Place the garlic on a sheet of aluminum foil and drizzle some olive oil on top, enough so that it seeps into the cloves.

4. Wrap aluminum foil tightly around the garlic, making sure no oil is leaking out. Roast it in the oven for 45 minutes.

5. When the garlic is roasted, allow it to cool, then unwrap the foil and begin pulling out the cloves using a small fork and your hands. They should be soft and easy to gently squeeze out.

6. Place the garlic and herbs in a small bowl and lightly press/mash everything against the side of the bowl to combine.

7. Mix in the oil and vinegar.

1 head of garlic

½ cup (125 ml) olive oil + extra for roasting garlic

Fresh basil to taste

Fresh rosemary to taste

¼ cup (60 ml) balsamic or red wine vinegar (choose your favorite)

2 ripe tomatoes, sliced

Salt and freshly cracked black pepper to taste

4 slices sourdough bread, toasted

Handful of wild arugula (optional)

Recipe continues...

8. Add the tomatoes, a pinch of salt, and a crack of pepper. If you can wait to eat, let this marinate for an hour.

9. Layer the garlic-and-herb mixture and tomatoes on the toast, and add the arugula if you're using it. Top with another sprinkle of salt and pepper, and you're done!

A NOTE ABOUT THIS RECIPE

The idea for this recipe was actually inspired by a friend in Hawaii. During a summer visit out there, I spent my last week with a school friend's older sister, who was also my babysitter's older sister. (Okay, I'm just trying to make things confusing now, right?) Basically, when I was growing up, a large family of mostly girls lived up the street from my family in Massachusetts. One ended up in Hawaii. I also ended up in Hawaii at one point. I stayed at her house, and we bought overpriced (but delicious) sourdough bread and she made this dish, or something very similar. It wasn't quite this, because I can't recall exactly what she put in it—but this is the taste my mouth remembers and celebrates. Getting away to Hawaii was good for me for a lot of reasons, but re-bonding with this friend and learning about new things to put on toast is pretty high up there on my treasured memories list.

TIP: If you're roasting one head of garlic, then why not two or three or even five? Roasted garlic is excellent for your health and fabulous for pastas, salad dressings, and life. Just be sure to consume it within the next day or two (which shouldn't be a problem, realistically).

KID-FRIENDLY TIP: Your kids probably won't be happy if you try to kiss them after eating this.

mushrooms with crispy sage

SERVES 2

I f you're a mushroom-lover looking for a recipe that's loaded with them, this is a delicious and luxurious choice. The trick to spectacular mushrooms is making sure to cook them properly. Nobody wants to bite down on a cold, squishy mushroom—it's just weird. An overcooked mushroom is better than a wet, soggy one, so make sure your skillet is hot and that you cook your mushrooms down until they begin to brown (or, if you're like me, really, really brown). Eating this dish, you'll fall in love with its savory richness and be surprised at how many mushrooms you can tuck away in one sitting. The truffle oil is optional; the dish is great without it, but it's absolutely amazing with that extra layer of flavorful, beneficial fat.

1 tablespoon dairy-free butter

One 14-ounce (400 g) package of mushrooms (any kind), sliced

About 20 sage leaves

Salt to taste

Olive oil to taste

2 thick slices sourdough bread

1 garlic clove, whole

Drizzle of truffle oil (optional, but highly recommended)

1. Melt the butter in a large skillet over medium-high heat.

2. Add the mushrooms and fry. Once the mushrooms have cooked down a bit, add the sage.

3. Allow the sage to get crispy in the skillet while the mushrooms continue to cook to a golden brown. Season with salt.

4. While the mushrooms cook, drizzle some olive oil on the bread, then toast in the oven.

5. After the bread is toasted, remove it from the oven and immediately, while the bread is still hot, smear the clove of garlic on top for flavor.

6. Top with the mushrooms and sage, and enjoy right away.

VARIATIONS:

If you're not into sage or don't have it on hand, rosemary makes a great replacement. And, like most things, this is also great with some avocado spread on top.

plantains & avocado

Have I mentioned yet how much I completely despise bananas? I really, truly do. I even have a hard time sitting near my own child when she's eating a banana. It's that bad. But you know what I do love? Really, truly love? A good fried (or baked) plantain—and this recipe is loaded with them. An added bonus: it's an easy way to use up leftover plantains. Enjoy this for breakfast, or serve it with black bean soup for lunch.

2 slices sourdough bread

Olive oil to taste

1 garlic clove, whole

1 very ripe plantain, sliced and baked or fried

1 Hass avocado, sliced or cubed

Cilantro, scallion, and/or chives to taste

Fresh lime juice to taste

Salt and black pepper to taste

Ghost pepper salt to taste (optional)*

1. Drizzle the bread with olive oil and toast it in the oven.

2. As soon as it's done toasting, rub the garlic clove on each slice of the toast for flavor.

3. Take a few slices of plantain and smash them onto the toast. Place some avocado on top, then garnish with the herbs.

4. Squirt some lime juice on top and season with salt and pepper. Serve!

*I'm a big fan of giving this a good sprinkle of ghost pepper salt, which is a specialty salt made with ghost chile peppers, to kick the toast up a notch, but that might just be me—I'm not sure how many people want to start their day off with a kick in the face from ghost peppers.

KID-FRIENDLY TIP: Skip the herbs to make the avocado and plantains the star!

A NOTE ABOUT THIS RECIPE

I'm pretty sure that Alex introduced me to this idea. I mean, he's definitely the one who keeps up the plantain demand in the kitchen—I use them, too, but he's ten times more likely to cut one open and cook it. It must have been years ago now, when we sat down to eat our typical breakfast (fruit, bread, and things to put on bread) and there were plantains included in the spread. I looked at him, confused. Plantains . . . without beans? What was happening? He said, "It's for the toast." And—boom—there it was: magic on toast. We don't make this all the time, but it's always a hit when we do. I love it, he loves it, and Marlowe loves it, too.

chocolate butter
& strawberries

You know what's fabulous? Chocolate. You know when chocolate is fabulous? Always. You know what's even more fabulous than chocolate all the time? When it's made to be incredibly healthy—but still richly indulgent—and it's slathered on warm, toasted bread. Everybody will love you for this. You'll love yourself for this. Hey, you'll love me for this. Protein, fiber, antioxidants, and chocolate. Honestly, I'm not even sure why you're still reading and not already in your kitchen making this recipe.

½ cup (60 g) raw cashews

8 pitted dates

8 tablespoons water + extra for soaking nuts and dates

½ cup (60 g) raw cacao nibs

2 tablespoons coconut oil (optional)

2 slices sourdough bread, toasted

Small handful of strawberries, sliced

1. Soak the cashews and dates in water for at least an hour, preferably overnight. Realistically, you don't have to soak them, but doing so cuts down tremendously on processing time and also makes the cashews more easily digestible.

2. Remove the cashews and dates from the water and place them in a food processor with the cacao nibs.

3. Slowly add the 8 tablespoons of water and process until the mixture is smooth, adding additional water or coconut oil if necessary.

4. Spread the chocolate mixture on the toast, then layer on some strawberries and feel good about eating chocolate for breakfast!

ROMANCE TIP: This could be the ultimate date-night dessert—the chocolate looks great on toast, but it's also amazing when you dip strawberries in it.

TIP FOR LEFTOVERS: Ha! Chocolate leftovers? Seriously, though: the sauce will harden when it cools, so if you want to eat it on toast the next day, just put some on the toast and plop it all right in the oven to heat up. This also makes a great base for a Chocolate Smoothie (page 286)!

cream cheese & roasted beets

SERVES 2

'll keep this one short and sweet: I love roasted beets with balsamic vinegar, and everything is better on toast.

1 medium red or gold beet

2 thick slices sourdough bread

Vegan cream cheese or other dairy-free substitute to taste

Honey or agave syrup to taste

Balsamic vinegar to taste

Salt to taste

1. Preheat the oven to 450°F (230°C).

2. Wrap the beet in aluminum foil and place it on a baking sheet. Roast for about 40 minutes, until tender.

3. Remove the beet from the oven and allow it to cool in the foil for at least 10 minutes. Once it's cool enough to handle, unwrap the foil and carefully peel the skin away. The beet will still be pretty warm, but you should be able to do this with your hands.

4. Toast your bread, then spread the cream cheese on the toast.

5. Slice the beet and layer it on top of the cream cheese.

6. Drizzle a generous amount of honey and a splash of balsamic vinegar on top, then sprinkle with some salt and devour.

TIP: This is best served while the beets are still warm.

sandwiches

a new take on a cucumber sandwich

MAKES 2 TO 3 SANDWICHES

When I first became pregnant, I could eat next to nothing, and I mean nothing. I lived off vegan cream cheese and cucumber sandwiches for the first few weeks. However, as I'm sure we all know, vegan cream cheese (or any cream cheese) probably isn't the best choice for a healthy diet—but it's darn good, right? Nothing really replaces it. Although the dill spread in this recipe isn't an exact substitute for cream cheese, it does give a really delectable twist to the traditional cream cheese sandwich. Plus it's unprocessed, contains protein, and, best of all—it's spicy! Your kids probably won't run after you begging for a spicy cucumber sandwich, so this is one of those things that's just for you. Make your sandwich, pour a glass of chilled wine or ice water, and sit back to enjoy, whether on your own or with friends. It's simple, distinct, and great for easy entertaining or for just having a moment to yourself.

SPICY DILL SPREAD

One 15-ounce (425 g) can chickpeas or white beans, drained well

2 tablespoons tahini

2 garlic cloves

6 tablespoons olive oil

1¼ teaspoons salt

3 tablespoons lemon juice

1 jalapeño, stemmed, seeded, and roughly chopped

1 packed tablespoon chopped dill

CUCUMBER SANDWICH

Table Bread (page 258) or bread of your choice

½ medium cucumber (preferably a super-crunchy one), thinly sliced

Salt to taste

Chopped dill to taste

1. Combine all the ingredients for the spread in a food processor and puree until smooth.

2. Layer a thick amount of the spread on two slices of bread.

3. Add a few layers of cucumbers to one side, then sprinkle on some salt and dill.

4. Close the sandwich and enjoy the spicy freshness.

TIP FOR LEFTOVERS: Use the spread as a veggie dip for a healthy snack option. It also makes a nutritious lunch in a wrap with sprouts, greens, and tomatoes. Yum!

chickpea salad sandwich

This recipe wears many delicious hats. It's incredible as a traditional sandwich, with bread surrounding its yummy insides, but I can serve the filling to Marlowe (and, let's be real, to myself, too) without the bread and still be just as pleased. Plus it travels well for picnics, school, work, etc. It's even great for breakfast!

Olive oil to taste

8 thick slices of sourdough bread

Handful of your favorite greens (we like to use arugula)

Chickpea Salad (recipe follows)

½ avocado, sliced

1 small apple (your favorite variety), thinly sliced

Fresh lemon juice to taste

Salt to taste

1. Drizzle some olive oil on each slice of bread, then toast them in the oven.

2. Layer the greens, Chickpea Salad, avocado, and apple on a slice of bread.

3. Squeeze some lemon on top and add a sprinkle of salt. Top with another slice of bread, and yum, yum, yum.

KID-FRIENDLY TIP: You can skip the onion if you'd like, though I do recommend keeping it in for flavor. I wouldn't skip the carrot, because it gives the chickpea salad a nice crunch. You can even chop up the apple and mix it into the chickpea salad to make it a bit easier to eat, since things tend to fall out of kids' sandwiches constantly—am I right?

chickpea salad

MAKES ENOUGH TO FEED ABOUT 4 PEOPLE, UNLESS YOU'RE
MARLOWE AND ME, IN WHICH CASE, 2 PEOPLE

¼ cup (60 g) vegan mayo

¼ cup (60 g) plain soy yogurt

1½ tablespoons apple cider vinegar

1½ teaspoons Dijon mustard

½ teaspoon salt

Black pepper to taste

One 15-ounce (425 g) can chickpeas,
drained

½ small onion, small diced
(about ¼ cup [40 g])

1 carrot, shredded
(about ½ packed cup [65 g])

1 tablespoon chopped dill

1. Combine all the wet ingredients in a medium bowl to create the dressing base. Season with salt and pepper.

2. In a large bowl, smash the chickpeas with a fork. You can leave a few chickpeas whole if you'd like, but mash most of them.

3. Mix the onion and carrot into the mashed chickpeas.

4. Combine the dressing with the chickpea and veggie mixture, then toss in the dill. You can serve this immediately, but allowing it to sit for at least an hour will make it taste even better.

lentil sloppy joes

Confession: I've only had "real" sloppy joes once in my life. I must have been seven or so, but I remember it pretty clearly. One of my parents' friends served it to me—I'm not sure if my mother even knows what a sloppy joe is. I sat at the table with this mess of a meal plopped on a bun in front of me, and I had a lot of questions. I couldn't wrap my head around the idea that it was supposed to be sloppy. Why would your parents want you to eat something so messy? Why would I want to eat something that chaotic? I don't remember the exact answer I was given, but it was something along the lines of "Why are you so picky? Just try the sandwich; it's good." Good might have been a stretch, but then again, I was never a big fan of beef, and I definitely never liked the unfamiliar. The truth is, I still don't really get the idea of a sloppy meal—what I do get, though, is that sauces can make or break a dish. And this crazy idea of a sandwich can work with a well-made sauce. The best news is you don't really have to "get it" to enjoy this. It just is what it is: a protein-packed, scrumptious, sauce-covered sandwich.

SLOPPY JOE BASE

2 tablespoons olive oil

1 small bell pepper, diced

1 small onion, diced

1 cup (190 g) dried green lentils

2 cups (500 ml) water

SLOPPY JOE SAUCE

½ cup (120 g) Ketchup (page 252)

1 tablespoon apple cider vinegar

1 teaspoon soy sauce

2 garlic cloves, minced

2 tablespoons tomato paste

1½ cups (350 ml) water

1. Heat the olive oil in a medium pot over medium heat.

2. Add the pepper and onion and sauté until tender and translucent.

3. Mix in the lentils and the water and simmer until the lentils are soft, about 20 to 25 minutes.

4. While the lentils are simmering, make your sauce by combining all the sauce ingredients in a medium pot and simmering over medium heat for 20 minutes.

5. When the lentils are done, mix the sauce together with the lentil mixture. Serve on toasted buns.

KID-FRIENDLY TIP: To turn this into a one-pot meal, serve the sloppy joe in bowls and throw some bread on the side. It makes cleanup slightly easier.

eggplant kimchi sandwich

MAKES 1 TO 2 SANDWICHES

This is basically a giant leftovers recipe—a mishmash of many delicious things made into a single extra-delicious thing. Leftover breaded eggplant? Kimchi in the fridge? Then you have the perfect makings for a sandwich party. Even if you don't have leftovers, it's worth it to make everything from scratch just to enjoy this sandwich.

Crusty baguette (mine is typically about 6 inches [15 cm] long)

A few tablespoons of Kimchi Mayo (recipe follows)

1 tablespoon olive oil

2 to 4 slices breaded eggplant (amount will depend on the size you want your sandwich to be—or how many leftovers you have!)

Fresh cilantro and mint to taste

1. Slice the baguette in half and toast it.

2. Slather on the Kimchi Mayo, letting the juices soak into the bread.

3. Heat the oil in a frying pan over medium-high heat.

4. Fry the breaded eggplant slices for about 3 minutes, until crispy. Flip them over and fry the other sides for another 3 minutes.

5. Construct your fried eggplant sandwich and garnish with herbs.

6. Eat and love eggplant.

KID-FRIENDLY TIP: The kimchi makes this sandwich not so kid-friendly, so you can try skipping that part and serving this with mayo or homemade Ketchup (page 252) instead.

eggplant
for everyone!

kimchi mayo

MAKE AS MUCH OR AS LITTLE
AS YOU WANT

Kimchi (page 250)

**Vegan mayo or other mayo
alternative**

Take equal parts of both ingredients
and mix. You can toss it all in a
food processor, or chop the kimchi
and mix it all together by hand
(so messy!). You won't need a lot
since a little goes a long way,
but oh boy is this delicious!

bánh mì chay

MAKES 1 TO 2 SANDWICHES

I f you've never had *bánh mì,* a type of Vietnamese sandwich, now is a great time to start. There's something special about Vietnamese places that offer this vegetarian version; unfortunately, they can be hard to find. Luckily, it's not difficult to make one at home.

French baguette

Vegan mayo or other mayo
    alternative to taste

A few slices of fried tofu,*
    ¼- to ½-inch (6 to 12 mm)
    thick

Very thinly sliced or
    mandoline-cut cucumber
    to taste (probably 4 to 6
    slices or so)

Pickled Daikon (page 249)
    and julienned carrots
    (use the daikon pickling
    sauce to pickle the carrots)
    to taste

A squeeze of lime

Sriracha to taste (optional)

1. Toast the baguette, then slice it open.

2. Spread on some mayo.

3. Pile on the other toppings and add a squeeze of lime. Sriracha is a great touch, too!

4. Enjoy your *bánh mì chay.*

* Extra-firm tofu works best in this recipe. Wrap the tofu in cloth and place a heavy object on top for about 20 minutes to drain the excess liquid, then slice it into ½-inch (12 mm) thick slabs and fry in oil for about 4 minutes on each side, until golden. You can also check out the super-easy "How to Fry Tofu" tutorial on my blog!

TIP FOR LEFTOVERS: Chop too many veggies or fry too much tofu? No worries! Make a deconstructed salad version for dinner or lunch the next day, or toss it all into a spring roll. Yum!

chay means
vegetarian in
Vietnamese.

our favorite veggie sandwich

MAKES 1 SANDWICH

W e're typically more of a "things on toast" kind of family (see page 61 for evidence), but everyone loves a good sandwich, and I love eating this sandwich with Alex and our little family. This recipe is truly our favorite, most simple bread-and-veggie recipe—one of the best things about it is that it's filling enough for even the hungriest of carnivores (ahem, Alex). Nothing about this recipe has been altered over the past six or so years that I've been making it. It doesn't need to change. And it's easy to increase the quantities to make more. Is it a big game day or a tailgating party? Better make 20!

Olive oil to taste

2 thick slices of sourdough bread

Hummus to taste

Sliced avocado to taste

A few pieces of thinly sliced cucumber or radish (for crunch!)

Small handful of peeled and grated beet

Small handful of grated carrot

1 small tomato (preferably heirloom), sliced

Handful of your favorite salad greens

Salt and black pepper to taste

Balsamic vinegar to taste

1. Drizzle the olive oil on the bread, then toast in the oven on one side.

2. Spread the hummus on the untoasted side of the bread.

3. Layer on the veggies and season with salt and pepper.

4. Add a drizzle of balsamic vinegar, then close your sandwich.

5. Welcome to the world of delicious raw beets.

TIP FOR LEFTOVERS: Shredded beets and carrots are always a great addition to a salad. Actually, anything and everything inside this sandwich can and should be used in your dinner salad—even the hummus works well in a dressing!

Recipe continues...

A NOTE ABOUT THIS RECIPE

Aren't they funny sometimes, the things that make you think of love? It's probably not a surprise, but for me it's often food that makes my heart sing with thoughts of my love for Alex. This sandwich is one of those foods.

Why does this sandwich inspire so much love in me? For a few reasons, really. I discovered the amazingness of shredded beets with Alex. A small restaurant we went to featured them in many of their recipes. Such a simple idea, yet such an amazing way to eat beets. Together we would visit the weekly markets for beets and any other ingredients we needed to create our own fresh, raw dishes. Sometimes Alex would even treat me to homemade bread.

Almost every day—often enough for me to become spoiled by it—he would make this sandwich for me while I was at work and walk it over to me. We'd sit together in a breezy walkway filled with wind chimes, tapestries, and hanging plants outside the sweaty, incense-filled hippie shop that I managed (I know . . . it's pretty amusing that I worked there, and it still amazes me when I think about it), and we would eat our sandwiches with chips. Always with chips.

snacks & appetizers

crispy fried chickpeas

Marlowe and I are big snackers. In fact, we fight over chips like it's our job—we don't have the best self-control when it comes to those—so we tend to keep them out of the house except for special occasions. Instead, when we're craving something salty and (lightly) fried, these chickpeas do the trick. Although you can roast chickpeas, cooking them in a skillet is much quicker and makes them taste even better—nice and crispy on the outside and not at all dry on the inside. Confession: Marlowe and I fight over these, too.

One 15-ounce (425 g) can chickpeas, rinsed and drained

1 tablespoon olive oil

¼ teaspoon salt

1 teaspoon nutritional yeast

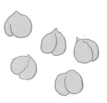

1. Dry the chickpeas—they don't have to be bone-dry, but you want to remove as much moisture as possible to make them extra-crispy.

2. Heat the oil in a medium pan or skillet over medium-high heat.

3. When the oil is very hot, add the chickpeas and let them cook for a few minutes until they begin to crisp a little bit.

4. Add the salt and toss carefully.

5. Continue frying the chickpeas until completely crispy, moving them as little as possible.

6. Gently stir in the nutritional yeast and fry for another minute.

7. Eat them as-is for a delicious little snack, or use them to garnish salad or soup, such as Creamy Butternut Squash & Kale Soup (page 130).

TIP: Don't stop at nutritional yeast—let your imagination go wild. Try a dash of tumeric, paprika, or curry on top.

lentil fritters

MAKES 12 TO 16 FRITTERS

If I could munch on these crispy little protein balls every day of my life, I would. When I make this recipe, I typically divide the batch in two: one half gets extra-spicy chiles mixed in; the other half goes without for the kiddo. You can use red or green lentils—both are delicious, and the only real difference will be the color. Do you want your fritters to be golden red or bright green? Your choice. Serve these hot off the stove, with yogurt or chutney (it's especially good with the Mango Chutney on page 248). Eat them as a fun snack or appetizer, or pair them with a full Indian feast.

2 cups (400 g) dried lentils, soaked overnight or for at least 3 hours

4 tablespoons grated or finely minced ginger

1 garlic clove

¾ teaspoon salt

½ bunch cilantro, roughly chopped, divided

1 teaspoon curry, paprika, or cumin (optional)

1 spicy chile, such as jalapeño, serrano, or habanero, small diced (optional)

1 small onion, diced

Canola or vegetable oil for frying

1. Drain the lentils from the soak water.

2. Blend the lentils, ginger, garlic, salt, and a handful of the cilantro in a food processor until mostly smooth.

3. Mix in the spices and chiles, if using.

4. In a large bowl, combine the lentil mixture with the diced onion and the remaining cilantro.

5. Heat about 2 inches (5 cm) of the oil in a medium pot over medium-high heat.

6. Using your hands, form the mixture into golf ball–size spheres and carefully drop them into the pot of hot oil. Fry for about 2 minutes on each side, until golden brown.

7. Remove the fritters from the pot and place them on a paper towel to allow the oil to drain off.

8. Serve immediately, with your favorite dipping sauce.

KID-FRIENDLY TIP: I like to keep big chunks of onion and cilantro in my fritters for flavor and texture, but feel free to leave those out if you want a lentil snack without the "pesky stuff" that sometimes scares kids.

spice it,
spice it real
good.

cauliflower & pea pockets

MAKES 8 POCKETS

While adults—or any mashed-potato lover, such as myself—will probably enjoy this dish, I more or less created it for the kiddo. I made the recipe super-easy, because the last thing busy people with children want is to spend hours in the kitchen. Plus it's an item picky eaters will embrace. What could be better than "mashed potatoes" (primarily cauliflower) in a crispy, handheld pocket?

3 cups (300 g) chopped cauliflower

1 cup (150 g) chopped potato (any variety)

4 tablespoons dairy-free butter (melted) or olive oil + extra for brushing on the phyllo

½ cup (80 g) nutritional yeast

1½ teaspoons salt

2 cups (280 g) fresh, frozen, or canned (and drained) peas

8 sheets phyllo dough, refrigerated until needed

1. Place the cauliflower and potato in a large pot and cover with water. Bring to a boil, then reduce to a simmer and cook until the vegetables are soft.

2. Once the potato and cauliflower are tender and easily pierce-able, drain the water and place them in a mixer to blend them or back into the pot to mash them by hand.

3. Add the butter, nutritional yeast, and salt and combine everything well, then stir in the peas and mix thoroughly.

4. Preheat the oven to 400°F (200°C).

5. Grab your phyllo dough from the fridge. You'll be working with one sheet of dough at a time, so be sure to cover the other sheets with a kitchen towel or plastic wrap so that they don't dry out.

6. Use a pastry brush to spread the melted butter (or olive oil) on the dough. Fold the sheet into thirds, creating one thick band. Brush with the melted butter again.

7. Place ⅓ to ½ cup (70 to 105 g) of the veggie mixture into the center of the folded sheet. Fold the top and bottom of the dough up to meet in the center, over the filling, then fold the remaining sides up one at a time to create a square-shaped pocket.

8. Brush melted butter (or olive oil) on both sides of the pocket and place it on a baking sheet. Repeat until all the filling has been used.

9. Bake for about 15 minutes, until golden. Best served warm and crisp out of the oven.

TIP FOR LEFTOVERS: Have extra filling left over? Serve it with Chickpea Patties (page 152) or another protein-filled dish and declare, "Dinner is ready."

kale & lentil spanakopita

I kept this dish light on spices for young taste buds, but don't confuse "light" with "boring" or "bland." These are sort of like a healthier, more delicate version of Empanadas (page 178), and they're easier to make, too, since you don't have to create the dough from scratch. They're so good for you, you can feel great about your other food choices for the week. Hooray!

2 tablespoons olive oil + extra for brushing the phyllo

1 large onion, diced or thinly sliced

5 garlic cloves, halved

1 teaspoon salt + extra for seasoning

1 teaspoon cumin seeds

1 head (about four handfuls) kale, stemmed and chopped

3 cups (700 ml) water or Vegetable Stock (page 116), divided

½ cup (100 g) dried green lentils (French lentils are fine, too—just don't use red lentils!)

1 teaspoon ground cumin

½ teaspoon ground sumac (optional)

½ cup (95 g) cooked quinoa

Black pepper to taste

10 to 12 sheets phyllo dough, refrigerated until needed

1. Place a large pot over medium heat. Add the oil and onion. Sauté until the onion is soft and translucent.

2. Mix in the garlic, salt, and cumin seeds. Stir until the seeds are toasted, adding a touch more oil if necessary.

3. Add the kale and sauté a bit, then add 1 cup (250 ml) water or stock and bring to a simmer. Cook until the kale is wilted and most of the liquid has evaporated.

4. Mix in the lentils and another 2 cups (500 ml) of the water or stock, then simmer over medium-low heat until the water has evaporated and the lentils are soft, about 20 minutes. Stir from time to time to make sure the lentils don't stick to the bottom of the pan.

5. Add the cumin powder and the sumac, if using. At this point your onion should be almost completely reduced and your garlic should practically melt into the other ingredients.

6. Add the cooked quinoa and mix. Season with salt and pepper.

7. Preheat the oven to 400°F (200°C).

Recipe continues...

8. Take out a sheet of phyllo dough, making sure to cover the other sheets with a kitchen towel or plastic wrap so that they don't dry out while you form the spanakopita.

9. Using a pastry brush, spread olive oil over the phyllo dough. Fold the sheet of phyllo dough in half, and then in half again, to create one long strip.

10. Place about ¼ cup (50 g) of the kale and lentil mixture about 2 inches (5 cm) in from one edge of the dough. Take the corner of that side and pull it up to meet the top of strip, creating a triangle shape. Continue to fold the triangle over itself until you reach the very end, completely wrapping the filling within the dough. Occasionally brush a bit of olive oil on the dough to help it stick together.

11. Once you've folded the triangle completely, all the ends should be thoroughly closed and the filling should be completely hidden inside. Brush some more olive oil on both sides of the pastry and place it on baking sheet.

12. Repeat steps 9 through 11 until the filling mixture is gone.

13. Sprinkle the triangles with a touch of salt and bake for about 15 minutes, until golden.

14. Savor.

TIP FOR LEFTOVERS: These are great for freezing! Just take any (cooled) leftovers and store them in a plastic freezer bag or wrapped in aluminum foil. Reheat in a 350°F (175°C) oven until completely warmed through, about 10 to 15 minutes, depending on the size.

mushroom pot stickers

MAKES 16 POT STICKERS

These yummy little pot stickers make a great healthy snack or supplement to a meal, and they're sure to impress your friends. They're completely worth the time it takes to prepare them. Even if they don't become a weekly addition to your meals, make sure to try them at least once—I promise you won't regret it!

1. Preheat the oven to 400°F (200°C).

2. Toss the mushrooms with the garlic, ginger, and 1 tablespoon of the olive oil, then season with salt and pepper.

3. Roast for 12 minutes, until the mushrooms have browned. Let cool before finely chopping them in a food processor.

4. Heat the remaining tablespoon of olive oil in a pan over low heat, and add the mushrooms and thyme. Slowly cook the mushrooms until all the liquid is evaporated, about 20 minutes.

5. Add the white wine and cook for another 10 minutes. Season with salt and pepper.

6. Mix in the rice vinegar and parsley, then allow the filling to cool.

7. To form the dumplings, place a tablespoon of the filling in the center of the wrapper. Wet all the edges with water.

8. Hold the dumpling with your thumb and middle finger, like a taco, using your index finger to keep the filling in place.

Recipe continues...

16 ounces (450 g) of your favorite fresh mushrooms (try a mixed variety!), scrubbed, cleaned, and sliced in half

3 garlic cloves, minced

One 1-inch (2.5 cm) piece of ginger, minced

2 tablespoons olive oil, divided

Salt and freshly cracked black pepper to taste

1 teaspoon chopped fresh thyme

½ cup (125 ml) dry white wine

1 teaspoon rice vinegar or sherry vinegar

1 tablespoon chopped fresh parsley

16 gyoza/pot sticker wrappers

2 tablespoons vegetable oil

⅓ cup (80 ml) water

THE PLANTIFUL TABLE

9. Pinch one end shut, then push the wrapper forward with your middle finger to pleat the top half of the dumpling and pinch it all the way shut. Continue to the end of the dumpling, using a final pinch to seal it tightly, and set it aside. Repeat this process until all the filling has been used.

10. Heat the vegetable oil in a large nonstick pan over medium heat. Place the dumplings in the pan and fry until the bottoms are golden.

11. Add the water to the pan, then cover and steam for 3 to 4 minutes, until the wrappers are soft.

12. Serve immediately with Citrus Ponzu (page 254) for dipping.

curried green veggie tempura

Hooray—tempura can be made egg-free! Now go eat some fried green veggies!

1 quart (950 ml) vegetable oil

1 cup (125 g) all-purpose flour, plus extra for dredging

1½ cups (350 ml) cold sparkling water

1 teaspoon salt, or to taste

¼ teaspoon turmeric

¼ teaspoon ground coriander

1 leek, trimmed, thoroughly cleaned, and cut into disks

Handful of fresh green beans

Handful of kale, very roughly chopped

Handful of non-watery salad leaves, such as arugula, amaranth, or a small mustard green

Freshly cracked black pepper to taste

Aïoli (recipe follows)

1. Heat the oil in a large pot over medium heat. Test whether the oil is hot enough by sticking the tip of a wooden chopstick into the oil. If bubbles form around it, the oil should be ready.

2. Combine the flour, water, salt, turmeric, and ground coriander in a large bowl. Stir until combined, making sure not to overmix.

3. Working in batches, dredge the vegetables first in flour and then in the batter, then place them in the hot oil one at a time.

4. When the tempura coating is crispy and golden, after 1 to 2 minutes, remove from the oil and drain on a paper towel.

5. Season generously with salt and pepper. Serve immediately with the Aïoli for dipping, and enjoy your fried veggies!

aïoli

MAKES ⅓ CUP (80 G)

⅓ cup (80 g) Veganaise
or other vegan mayonnaise

Juice and zest of 1 lemon

Combine both ingredients. Refrigerate until
needed.

TIP FOR LEFTOVERS: The Aïoli
dip is also really good with the
Chickpea or Hearts of Palm
Patties (page 152 or 154).

carrot bites

MAKES 15 TO 20 CARROT BITES

A favorite food of kiddos everywhere, reinvented. These protein-packed little nuggets have a sweet, soft inside with a nice, crispy outside. A note, though: they aren't supposed to mimic meat, so you won't be able to tell kids, "They're just like chicken nuggets." They'll enjoy them nonetheless. No children around? Try adding a dash of ginger and serving them with a sweet-and-sour dipping sauce for yourself (some kids might like that, too!). Any way you enjoy them, it feels good to make bite-size kid food and skip the processed options.

CARROT MIXTURE

- 5 to 6 medium carrots (any color), quartered
- 1 to 2 tablespoons olive oil + more for baking
- 1 to 2 garlic cloves
- 1 cup (200 g) pressed, drained, and crumbled firm or extra-firm tofu
- 1 cup (273 g) cooked quinoa
- 1½ teaspoons salt

BREADING

- ½ cup (62 g) all-purpose flour
- 1 cup (250 ml) almond milk or water
- ½ cup (40 g) nutritional yeast
- 1 cup (110 g) dried bread crumbs
- ½ cup (93 g) cooked quinoa
- ½ teaspoon salt

1. Preheat the oven to 450°F (230°C).

2. Place the carrots on a baking sheet and drizzle olive oil over them. Toss the carrots to coat them completely with oil. (It may seem silly to use a whole baking sheet for just six carrots, but you'll need the sheet later in the recipe, so my method is to dirty one now and re-use it rather than dirtying extra dishes.)

3. Bake for about 15 minutes, then remove the sheet from the oven and toss the carrots around on the sheet a bit. Place them back in the oven and continue baking for another 10 minutes or so, until the carrots are completely tender. The total cooking time will vary depending on size of the carrots, but it'll typically be between 20 and 35 minutes.

4. While the carrots are roasting, combine the garlic, tofu, ½ cup (93 g) quinoa, and 1½ teaspoons salt in a food processor.

5. Remove the roasted carrots from the oven. Leave the oven on since you'll be baking your carrot bites in there.

6. Add the carrots to the tofu and quinoa mixture in the food processor and puree everything completely.

Recipe continues...

snack time!

7. Coat the baking sheet with a generous amount of olive oil and set it aside for later.

8. Add another ½ cup (95 g) quinoa to the food processor and pulse a few times to combine.

9. Place the mixture in a large bowl and set it aside on the counter while you prepare the breading.

10. Get out three separate shallow bowls. Fill one bowl with flour and another bowl with milk. Combine the nutritional yeast, bread crumbs, ½ cup (93 g) quinoa, and ½ teaspoon salt in the last bowl.

11. Take the carrot mixture and begin making small nugget shapes—the breading will bulk it up a bit, so you don't need much to make a nice, plump nugget; about 1 to 1½ tablespoons should do the trick.

12. Being careful not to squeeze or smush your shape, place the nugget in the flour bowl and coat it on all sides, then very quickly dunk it in the milk, and then in the bread-crumb mixture. Make sure the nugget is completely coated, then place it on the oiled baking sheet.

13. Repeat steps 11 and 12 until you've used the entire mixture.

14. Bake the nuggets for about 8 minutes on each side (16 minutes total), flipping them when golden.

15. Serve them with your favorite dipping sauce, such as honey mustard or Ketchup (page 252).

salads
& sides

coleslaw

Marlowe is obsessed with this stuff. Every time she sees a head of cabbage, she begs me to make coleslaw. (It's really kind of crazy how into it she is.) Coleslaw—creamy, crunchy, summertime side dish of champions—oh, how my child loves you. We eat it as a midday snack or occasionally pair it with Vegetable & Bean Chili (page 136) and Plantain Corn Bread (page 262). It's the perfect side dish to bring to a summer party or to pack for a picnic, or you can be like us and eat it immediately, fighting over who gets to make and taste-test the sauce.

½ cup (120 g) vegan yogurt

½ cup (120 g) vegan mayo

½ teaspoon Dijon mustard

2 tablespoons apple cider vinegar

Juice of ½ lemon (about 1 tablespoon)

1 small head of cabbage, thinly sliced

Two carrots, grated

Handful of radishes (I like to use the Easter Egg variety for a fun color), thinly sliced into matchsticks

Salt and black pepper to taste

1. Combine the wet ingredients together to create the dressing.

2. Mix the vegetables together in a large bowl. Toss the dressing with the vegetables until everything is evenly coated. Season with salt and pepper.

3. Let sit for an hour, then enjoy!

KID-FRIENDLY TIP: Use purple cabbage rather than green cabbage to increase the color factor. Or you can try adding a small raw shredded beet to the mix. Pink-and purple-lovers of all ages will "oooh" and "ahhh" at this bright and colorful dish.

ah, refreshing.

butter bean & quinoa salad

SERVES 2

Although I'm generally more of a comfort-food type of person, some days I want nothing more than a refreshing salad. This is one of my recipes for those times.

1. Combine all the ingredients for the dressing in a small bowl and mix until smooth.

2. Toss the salad ingredients together in a large bowl.

3. Mix the dressing together with the vegetables. This tastes great served cold or at room temperature.

KID-FRIENDLY TIP: Cook the pepper and onion first, or skip them altogether.

TIP FOR LEFTOVERS: Mix any leftovers into a simple kale salad for an added crunch.

DRESSING

1 garlic clove

½ teaspoon salt

½ Hass avocado or ¼ small Florida avocado, mashed

1 teaspoon olive oil

1 tablespoon apple cider vinegar

2 tablespoons water

SALAD

½ cup (93 g) cooked quinoa

½ cup (90 g) small diced bell pepper

¼ cup (40 g) small diced red onion

1 cup (75 g) canned butter beans (lima beans), drained and rinsed

bread salad

With a garden out back, we find ourselves eating salads pretty often. A basic version with greens (we like arugula), thinly sliced veggies, and Sherry Vinaigrette (page 241) will always hit the spot when we're looking for a light lunch on a hot day. When you add sourdough bread to the mix (a fancy crouton, really)—*bam*—instant goodness. Even Marlowe loves to dig into this. The bread can be as crispy as you want. I like it different ways, from lightly toasted to majorly crunchy, depending on my mood and what I'm craving. The real secret is making sure the bread gets a nice coating of dressing when you toss the salad.

¼ loaf day-old sourdough bread, cut into 1-inch (2.5 cm) squares

A few drizzles of olive oil for coating the bread

A pinch of salt

A few sprigs of fresh thyme

Two handfuls of salad greens

1 heirloom tomato, cut into 1-inch (2.5 cm) cubes or thinly sliced

Small handful of radishes, thinly sliced

Small handful of fresh chopped herbs, such as basil and oregano

Sherry Vinaigrette (page 241)

1. Preheat the oven to 450°F (230°C).

2. Toss the bread with the olive oil, salt, and thyme in a medium bowl.

3. Toast the bread until golden brown.

4. Toss the salad ingredients with the toasted bread and vinaigrette. Serve immediately.

THE PLANTIFUL TABLE

coconut & mango noodle salad

SERVES 2

Make this whenever you want to feel like you're on a tropical vacation.

1. Mix the first six ingredients together in a large bowl until well blended.

2. Add the noodles and gently toss.

3. Gently mix in the remaining ingredients, then serve.

KID-FRIENDLY TIP: This is already pretty child-friendly, but you can adjust the veggies you use to meet your kiddo's wants and needs.

1 tablespoon grated ginger

½ cup (125 ml) coconut milk

1 teaspoon lemon juice

1 ⅓ teaspoons rice vinegar or apple cider vinegar

2½ teaspoons honey or agave syrup

1 tablespoon soy sauce

4 ounces uncooked vermicelli rice noodles, prepared as directed and cooled

½ bell pepper, julienned

1 small chayote squash, julienned

1 small unripe mango, julienned

¼ head of small cabbage, thinly sliced

roasted vegetable salad for all seasons

SERVES 4 AS A SIDE DISH

Alex and I have been making this salad for years. It's a great choice to bring to holiday dinners, or to enjoy on days when you're craving a hearty salad but it's a bit too cold out for the typical cold, raw veggie salad. This is so delicious, just thinking about it makes my mouth water!

15 to 20 baby carrots

1 medium or large beet, sliced

Handful of small radishes (about 10)

1 fennel bulb, sliced

Olive oil for roasting

Salt to taste

Fresh thyme to taste

Fresh rosemary to taste

Two handfuls of your favorite hearty salad greens (baby kale or arugula work great)

Balsamic Vinaigrette (page 240) to taste

Freshly cracked black pepper to taste

1. Preheat the oven to 450°F (230°C).

2. Lay out all your root vegetables (not the greens) on a baking sheet. Drizzle them with olive oil, then sprinkle on some salt, thyme, and rosemary (you can leave the stems on). Toss the vegetables to coat them in the oil and herbs and spread them evenly across the sheet.

3. Cook for about 30 minutes, until all the vegetables are soft and easily pierce-able. Make sure to toss your vegetables around on the sheet about 10 minutes into the roasting time.

4. Remove the veggies from the oven and allow them to cool. Once they're cool enough to handle, mix them with the greens and a bit of Balsamic Vinaigrette (page 240). Sprinkle with salt and pepper and serve warm.

cooked kale

Marlowe fell in love with this recipe as soon as I started making it. Then over time the dish fell out of rotation, and months (maybe a year) went by before I made it again. I was nervous that maybe my daughter's taste buds had changed. Or would her toddler skepticism get in the way? I showed her a photo to prove that, at one point in her life, she had adored kale. She gave me a bit of a side-eye but agreed to give the stuff a taste. With two little fingers she picked up a clump of kale, popped it into her mouth, and started chewing. Then she looked up at me with bright eyes and said, "It's juicy! I like it." It's still a winner to this day. Hooray for kale!

2 teaspoons olive oil

1 medium onion, diced

4 cloves of garlic, chopped

2 bunches of kale, stemmed
   and roughly chopped

1 teaspoon salt

2 tablespoons apple cider
   vinegar

1 teaspoon liquid smoke

3 cups (700 ml) Vegetable
   Stock (page 116)

1. Heat the olive oil in a large pot over medium-high heat.

2. Cook the onion until soft and translucent.

3. Toss in the garlic and cook for another 30 seconds to 1 minute.

4. Add the kale and a splash of water and stir. In a matter of minutes the kale will begin to wilt and cook down. When that happens, stir in the salt.

5. Stir in the vinegar, liquid smoke, and vegetable stock and simmer over medium-low heat for 25 to 30 minutes, until the kale is soft and the stock has reduced almost entirely. Serve hot.

A NOTE ABOUT THIS RECIPE

You know what's awesome about blogging? Not just sharing your story and what you know,
but having people share their world back. When I first decided to put this recipe out there,
I was nervous that everyone would roll their eyes at me, like, "Okay, great—your kid eats kale,
but mine won't!" But then the opposite happened, and emails and comments poured in, with
mothers letting me know the great news about their children eating kale. I was excited; it
turns out other people's kids love this, too! It makes me so happy to hear that I'm helping kids
everywhere learn to eat, and enjoy, kale.

roasted baby artichokes

This recipe is simply and utterly delicious. Baby artichokes aren't the easiest thing to find here in Florida, but when we do get a hold of them, we always make this dish.

2 lemons

16 baby artichokes

4 garlic cloves

1 teaspoon salt, or to taste

Handful of fresh herbs
(thyme, rosemary, parsley,
cilantro, oregano, basil—
whatever suits your tastes)

¼ cup (60 ml) olive oil

Zest of 1 lemon

Freshly cracked black pepper
to taste

1. Preheat the oven to 500°F (260°C).

2. Squeeze the juice from the lemons into a large bowl filled with cold water.

3. Remove the outer leaves of the artichokes, then trim the bases and stems with a peeler and cut off the top third of the artichoke.

4. Slice the artichokes in half and place them into the lemon water. Set aside.

5. Use a mortar and pestle to crush the garlic and salt into a paste. Add the herbs and mash into a chunky paste, then add the olive oil, lemon zest, and pepper and mix until combined.

6. Drain the water from the artichokes and place them in a large bowl. Toss them with the herb mixture.

7. Spread the artichokes out in an even layer on a baking sheet. Roast for 15 minutes, until they have deepened in color, tossing them halfway through the cooking time.

8. Season lightly with salt before serving.

TIP FOR LEFTOVERS: Add these little guys to a salad (try the Roasted Vegetable Salad for All Seasons on page 106) or pasta (such as the Lemony Vegetable & Herb Pasta on page 220).

eggplant mashed potatoes

SERVES 4 AS A SIDE DISH

Eggplant mashed potatoes? Sounds a little crazy, right? Trust me—they're not! This recipe is perfection, as well as a wonderfully creative way of hiding extra veggies inside a well-loved dish. The inspiration for this was sort of random: I once had a comment on my blog about putting tahini in mashed potatoes. Months and months later, while I was cooking, my mind jumped back to that comment. My taste buds and brain went from tahini to hummus to babaganoush to eggplant to "Hey! That might not be too bad!" And it wasn't too bad—in fact, it was awesome! Just make sure you roast the eggplant to complete creaminess, and you'll have yourself a surprisingly delicious side dish featuring a double dose of vegetables.

1 small eggplant, halved

Olive oil for roasting

1 teaspoon salt + more for baking eggplant

3 medium creamer potatoes, chopped

2 tablespoons dairy-free butter

Splash of dairy-free milk (optional)

Freshly cracked black pepper to taste

1. Preheat the oven to 400°F (200°C).

2. Brush the flesh side of the eggplant with olive oil and sprinkle it with salt.

3. Place the eggplant halves peel side down on a baking sheet and cook for 30 to 40 minutes (depending on the size), until the insides are very, very tender. Pierce through the top to test the inside; the softer, the better.

4. While the eggplant is roasting, place the potatoes in a medium pot and cover them with water. Bring to a boil, then simmer until the potatoes are soft.

5. Drain the water from the potatoes and place them in a large bowl. Remove the peel, if you prefer.

6. Scoop out the inside of the eggplant and place it in the mixing bowl with the potato. Discard the peel.

7. Whip the potatoes, eggplant, butter, and salt together until smooth and creamy. Add a splash of milk, if necessary.

8. Season with salt and pepper.

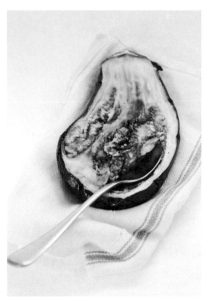

A NOTE ABOUT THIS RECIPE

While I don't like to rely on "hidden vegetable" meals, since I think kids should learn to love every vegetable on its own (okay, well, maybe not every one), sometimes they are the quickest way to get your kid to start eating less-palatable veggies. This dish works like a charm.

TIP: Garlic mashed potatoes? Yes, please! Since you'll be heating up the oven to cook the eggplant anyway, consider roasting a whole head of garlic, too, and mixing it in with the potatoes (see page 55 for instructions on roasting garlic).

KID-FRIENDLY TIP: Nutritional yeast, always and forever. A sad day for Marlowe involves mashed potatoes without it. Throw in a tablespoon when you whip the potatoes.

fragrant stir-fried cauliflower

This works as a wonderful side dish for many occasions—and with all the veggies and just a touch of sugar, it almost gets an A+ for healthiness, too.

¼ cup (60 ml) rice vinegar

2 teaspoons sugar

½ teaspoon soy sauce

¼ teaspoon sambal (chile pepper sauce)

1 tablespoon water

1 tablespoon vegetable oil

1 teaspoon minced garlic

1 teaspoon minced ginger

1 teaspoon minced lemongrass

1 chile pepper (jalapeño or Thai chile are both great options), sliced

¼ head of cauliflower, thinly sliced

¼ cup (30 g) roasted cashews

¼ cup (35 g) pumpkin seeds

1 tablespoon sunflower seeds

Pinch of salt

Chopped fresh mint and cilantro to taste

Lime wedges to taste

1. Combine the vinegar, sugar, soy sauce, sambal, and water in a small bowl. Stir until the sugar is fully dissolved, then set aside.

2. Place a well-seasoned wok over high heat.

3. Add the vegetable oil and the garlic, ginger, lemongrass, and chile pepper. Stir-fry for about a minute, until toasted and fragrant.

4. Mix in the cauliflower and stir-fry for a few minutes, until tender and slightly charred.

5. Add the cashews and the seeds and stir-fry another minute or so, then remove from the heat.

6. Toss the mixture with the sauce you prepared in step one, along with the mint and cilantro.

7. Serve immediately, garnished with fresh lime.

soups,
stews, &
savory
pies

vegetable stock

Although it's incredibly easy to buy pre-made vegetable stock, it's also incredibly easy and economical to make your own at home. Plus there's something so rewarding about using a homemade stock in your recipes.

4 quarts (3.8 L) cold water

3 onions

2 carrots

2 celery stalks

¼ cup (7.5 g) dried mushrooms (any variety)

4 slices of sun-dried tomatoes

Outer leaves of 1 artichoke

1 teaspoon peppercorns

6 sprigs of fresh thyme

Handful of fresh parsley

1. Combine all the ingredients in a large stockpot over medium to medium-high heat.

2. Bring the mixture to a simmer and cook for 30 to 40 minutes.

3. Strain the stock liquid and allow it to cool. Refrigerate until needed.

TIP: It can feel pretty crummy to throw out all those leftover veggie scraps after you strain the stock, especially if you don't compost, so here's an idea if you have a canine pal and feel up to it: pick out all the onions and use the scraps for Homemade Dog Food (page 294)!

TIP FOR LEFTOVERS: Place the stock back into the pot and cook it a bit longer to reduce the liquid even more and enhance the flavor. Cool the reduced stock and pour it into ice-cube trays or small freezer-safe containers to freeze. Just pop out the blocks of frozen stock and defrost to use in your recipe as needed. *Boom*—you never have to make a last-minute trip to the store for stock again.

good for
the soul.

marlowe's favorite green soup

SERVES 3 TO 4

My biggest nightmare as a kid was my mom's once-weekly "green soup." Even though she put every topping imaginable (cheese, chips, whatever) on that bowl of creamy soup to try to convince me to eat and love it, I hated that stuff, no matter what. My mother, with great certainty, told me that I should expect to grow up and struggle with picky eaters of my own. And now here I am with a daughter of my own, and you know what? Her favorite soup is "green soup." Although my recipe is different than my mom's less vegetable-heavy version, the care and love that go into it are the same.

1 tablespoon dairy-free butter or olive oil

1 small to medium onion, chopped

3 medium potatoes, chopped (any creamy kind; not Idaho)

3 to 4 cups (264 to 352 g) chopped fresh or frozen broccoli*

1 teaspoon salt, or to taste

About 2½ cups (625 ml) water or Vegetable Stock (page 116)

2 heaping tablespoons nutritional yeast, or to taste

Freshly cracked black pepper to taste

1. Heat the butter or oil in a large pot over medium heat.

2. Add the onion and cook until translucent.

3. Mix in the vegetables and salt.

4. Add enough water or stock to cover the vegetables and simmer until the potatoes and broccoli are very tender. To check for doneness, occasionally pierce the potato with a fork; if the potato slips off, it's done.

5. Toss in the nutritional yeast.

6. Puree everything, slowly adding enough liquid to create a smooth and creamy consistency.

6. Season with salt and pepper, then enjoy your green soup!

Despite Marlowe and Alex's fondness for broccoli, it isn't an everyday vegetable in our home, so I find it much easier to buy frozen broccoli than fresh. It works just as well, and you don't really have to worry about it going bad.

KID-FRIENDLY TIP: This soup (like many soups) freezes beautifully. I like to stick kid-size portions in the freezer to use on days that I don't have much time to cook but still want Marlowe to eat a healthy meal. Simply place it in a freezer-safe container (make sure to leave room for liquid expansion) and freeze. Defrost the soup by placing the container in a warm bowl of water, or use a microwave, before reheating it on the stove. Add a small amount of water if necessary.

TIP FOR LEFTOVERS: If you ever find yourself with too many leftover mashed potatoes (yeah, right), use them in place of the whole potatoes for this soup. Simmer the broccoli and add the mashed potatoes in just before blending.

P.S.: Thanks for caring about me enough to always force me to eat green soup, Mom.

split pea soup

This is one of those meals that's easy to live off of when you need to, since it costs almost nothing to make and is incredibly filling. (Trust me, I've done it.) And if you make the vegetable stock yourself or skip it completely and use water, it costs just pennies per bowl. Not only is this soup economical, it's filled with fresh vegetables and lots of protein. Whether you decide to puree it to a smooth texture or not, this meal won't leave you hungry. It's perfect for all seasons—including the short-on-cash season—and is especially soothing on chillier days. How comforting to know that you've created a healthy, hearty, and tasty meal out of very little.

1 tablespoon olive oil

1 large onion, diced

2 celery stalks, diced

2 carrots, diced

1 to 3 garlic cloves, minced

2 medium creamer potatoes, diced or cubed

1½ cups (300 g) dried split peas (green or yellow)

7 cups (1.7 L) Vegetable Stock (page 116)

2 teaspoons salt, divided

1 teaspoon liquid smoke, or to taste*

Black pepper to taste

1. Lightly coat the bottom of a large pot with the olive oil and place over medium-high heat. Add the onion and celery and cook until translucent and soft.

2. Mix in the carrots and cook for another 2 minutes, then add the garlic and stir for 30 seconds.

3. Mix in the potatoes, split peas, vegetable broth, 1 teaspoon salt, and liquid smoke.

4. Bring everything to a boil, then lower to a simmer. Simmer for 40 minutes, stirring occasionally, especially toward the end since this is when the soup may start sticking to the bottom.

5. At the end of 40 minutes, stir in a splash of liquid smoke and another teaspoon of salt and stir well. The soup will have a nice, thick consistency, but if you prefer a thinner soup you can add up to 1 cup (250 ml) of additional stock or water. You can also puree this if you like, but you may need to add another splash of stock if you do so.

6. Season with pepper and remaining salt and serve.

Traditional split pea soup contains a lot of pork products. By adding a touch of liquid smoke instead, you take out the extra cholesterol and fat to get a lean, fiber-filled, and still protein-packed dish.

TIP: Sometimes I like to garnish this with a splash of lemon juice, olive oil, and cayenne pepper—it really takes it up a notch!

KID-FRIENDLY TIP: Reduce this down even more to make a nourishing and filling baby or toddler meal.

TIP FOR LEFTOVERS: This soup is freezable, but you may need to add a decent amount of stock to bring it back to life the next time you serve it. To defrost, simply leave the soup on the counter until thawed, then reheat it on the stove, or you can speed up the process by placing the entire container in a large bowl of hot water. I also recommend pureeing it when you reheat it, if you haven't done so already, which will provide a better texture.

creamy tomato soup

SERVES 4

We have two variations of tomato soup in our house. One is chunky and full of flavorful broth (see the Bread Soup on page 124), and the other one, this one, is smooth and luscious. This creamy version isn't just the chunky soup blended up—they're actually completely different. This one is a hit with everyone, while the Bread Soup is a bit more suited to tomato-loving grown-ups and kids. We like to match this with a grilled cheese sandwich and some chips or maybe a salad, depending on how healthy and light we want to be.

3 tablespoons olive oil

1 large onion, diced

3 celery stalks, diced

1 leek, cut in half and sliced

2 carrots, diced

4 garlic cloves, sliced

½ cup (23 g) fresh basil leaves

4 sprigs of fresh oregano, roughly chopped

4 sprigs of fresh thyme, leaves only

1 sprig of fresh rosemary, leaves only

2 teaspoons salt

Freshly cracked black pepper to taste

One 28-ounce (794 g) can of whole peeled tomatoes

Empty tomato can filled with water (3½ cups or 794 ml)

1. Heat the olive oil in a heavy-bottomed pot or Dutch oven over medium heat. Cook the onion, celery, leek, and carrots until translucent, about 10 minutes.

2. Add the garlic and cook for a few more minutes, then mix in the herbs and cook for another minute or so, until very fragrant. Season with salt and pepper.

3. Add the can of tomatoes and the water. Simmer for 30 minutes, taste, and adjust seasoning if necessary.

4. Puree until smooth and serve immediately.

KID-FRIENDLY TIP (FOR LEFTOVERS): Serve this as a sauce with pasta. Recommended for when you're in a pinch and trying to feed a kid. Not recommended for when you're trying to impress guests.

bread soup

Alex and I could argue for hours about who created this soup. I'll claim ownership to my grave, but part of my gut second-guesses it. Realistically, I think this is how the story goes: I fell in love with Alex because of his soup. (Okay, fine, I fell in love with him because of his pizza, but let's continue the story, anyway.) His soups are really, really impressive. Tomato soup was the first meal he ever made for me, and I asked for it all the time after that. I'm a creature of habit, so when he added bread to our soup one time, I was absolutely thrown off and, honestly, almost uneasy. I wanted my bread next to my soup—not in it. Why on earth would he put my bread in my tomato soup? As it turns out, there's really no going back after that happens. It was good. Incredibly good. I liked Alex's idea so much that I decided to create something else that was similar to tomato soup, but different enough to be a completely new addition to our soup rotation. This does feature tomatoes, but the main stars (besides the bread, of course) are the paprika and garlic. So, who created this dish? I say me. But I do thank Alex for wooing me with his bread soup.

1 pint (285 g) grape or cherry tomatoes

1 head of garlic, peeled and roughly chopped (keep two cloves intact)

Salt to taste

Handful of fresh basil, divided

2 tablespoons olive oil, divided

1 small to medium onion, minced

1½ teaspoons sweet smoked Spanish paprika

1 tablespoon minced oregano

½ cup (126 g) tomato puree

5 to 6 cups (1.2 to 1.4 L) Vegetable Stock (page 116)

About ¼ loaf sourdough bread (exact amount will depend on your bread cravings and the size of your loaf), cut or torn into 2-inch (5 cm) pieces

Black pepper to taste

1. Heat the oven to 450°F (230°C).

2. In a large oven-safe dish, combine the cherry tomatoes, half of the chopped garlic (about 5 cloves), a generous amount of salt, and a few of the basil leaves. Add 1 tablespoon olive oil and mix, coating everything with the oil. Roast in the oven until the tomatoes are nicely wrinkled and blistered.

3. While the tomatoes are roasting, heat 1 tablespoon of the olive oil in large pot over medium heat. Add the onion and sauté until translucent. Stir in the paprika, coating the onion.

4. Mix in the remaining garlic (chopped and whole cloves) and season with salt. Sauté for another minute, then add the oregano and remaining basil and give it a quick stir.

5. Stir in the tomato puree and stock. Add the roasted tomatoes and any oil, garlic, and juices that are left in the roasting pan. Simmer for 15 to 20 minutes.

6. Add chunks of bread—as much or as little as you like*—and simmer on low for another minute. Season with salt and pepper before serving.

The amount we add depends on our mood and the weather. There's something very cozy about a thick and hearty bread soup in the winter, but a lighter soup is nicer in the hot summer months.

KID-FRIENDLY TIP: There's a lot of garlic in this one, so if you don't regularly feed your children heavy doses of garlic the way we do, then it might be a bit tough for them to digest. Although this isn't actually a tip on how to feed this soup to your kids, it's a word of caution for little tummies.

potato leek soup

Making potato leek soup isn't rocket science—in fact, it's one the tastiest, most user-friendly soups around. If it weren't for the whole "using fire" aspect to cooking, Marlowe could make this recipe. But, in her own words, "I can't make soup; I'm not allowed to use the stove." Well, kid, if you could reach high enough and use the stove safely, you could make this, even at three years old. And, of course, any adult can and should make this, too.

2 to 3 large or 4 to 5 small leeks, dark green stems removed, leeks cut lengthwise down the middle and washed very well—they can be **rather dirty veggies**

2 tablespoons dairy-free butter or olive oil

3 medium creamer potatoes, chopped

1 teaspoon salt, or to taste

Black pepper to taste

Vegetable Stock (page 116) or water

⅓ cup (53 g) nutritional yeast (optional)

1. After thoroughly washing your leeks, slice them into half rings.

2. Melt the butter in a large pot over medium heat.

3. Add the leeks and cook, stirring occasionally, until they've have completely cooked down.

4. Mix in the potatoes, salt, and pepper.

5. Add enough vegetable stock or water to cover the leeks and potatoes.

6. Simmer until the potatoes are completely tender and almost breaking apart.

7. Stir in the nutritional yeast and allow the soup to simmer for another minute.

8. Do a taste-test, adding more salt if necessary. Serve and enjoy!

KID-FRIENDLY TIP: This is about as kid-friendly as it gets—but, chances are, your kid will like it pureed, not chunky.

- Puree the soup completely, adding additional stock as necessary, for a very creamy and delicious soup.
- Toss in some canned (drained and rinsed) chickpeas at the same time as the potatoes for a chunky, protein-filled soup.
- Puree everything and add half an avocado and the juice of half a lemon. Allow it to cool completely and serve cold, with an extra crack of freshly ground pepper.

chunky

pureed

corn & potato chowder

SERVES 4

"Ah, potatoes and corn," my husband jokingly says when I make this chowder, "the two things you Colombians love most." He's right; they're both a pretty big staple in the Colombian diet. I find his statement funny, though, because, to me, this dish is such an American idea. Although it doesn't contain enough vegetables for me to consider it a "healthy" meal it's filling, delicious, and great for a summer or winter day—or fall or spring, too, really.

3 cups (750 ml) warm, unflavored almond milk, divided

3 small corn tortillas (we typically use the store-bought ones we have sitting in fridge, or you can try the homemade ones on page 264)

1 tablespoon dairy-free butter or olive oil

1 large onion, small diced

1 celery stalk, small diced

¾ cup (125 g) chopped smoked tempeh

2 creamer potatoes, small diced

2 cups (320 g) fresh or frozen corn

1½ teaspoons salt, divided

1 cup (250 ml) Vegetable Stock (page 116)

Freshly cracked pepper to taste

1. In a small bowl, combine 1 cup (250 ml) warm almond milk with the tortillas and set aside to soak.

2. Heat the butter or oil in a large pot over medium heat.

3. Add the onion and celery and cook until translucent.

4. Mix in the tempeh and cook until crisp, 1 to 2 minutes.

5. Stir in the potatoes, corn, and ½ teaspoon salt.

6. Add the vegetable stock and simmer over low heat until the potatoes are tender.

7. As soon as the soup begins to simmer, blend the tortilla and milk mixture until very smooth, either using an immersion blender or transferring it to a standing blender. Set aside.

8. When the potatoes are tender, add the (now thickened) tortilla mixture and stir well.

9. Add the remaining 2 cups (500 ml) of milk, another teaspoon of salt, and a few good cracks of pepper. Allow the soup to simmer for another minute or two before serving.

TIP: This tastes wonderful with a jalapeño or other spicy pepper. Just dice it up and add it in with the onion and celery. It won't be kid-friendly, but it will be absolutely delicious.

creamy butternut squash & kale soup

SERVES 4

We call this "orange soup." I originally posted a variation of this recipe on my blog as a carrot soup, but as time passed I altered it, first into a smoky sweet potato soup, and now here as a (still smoky) butternut squash soup. Our recipes change depending on the season and what we have in abundance, but any of the wonderful vegetables I've just mentioned work beautifully in this soup. You'll find that butternut squash creates a lighter dish, whereas sweet potatoes or carrots lend a bit more heartiness. Choose your favorite, or use whatever's in your fridge!

1½ tablespoons olive oil

1 medium onion, diced

2 carrots, diced

1 celery stalk, diced

Pinch of chili flakes (optional)

1 small butternut squash, peeled, de-seeded, and cubed

¼ teaspoon cumin

¾ teaspoon sweet smoked Spanish paprika

2 teaspoons salt

Vegetable Stock (page 116) or water

¼ teaspoon liquid smoke

1½ packed cups roughly chopped kale

Juice of ½ lemon (about 1 tablespoon)

Freshly cracked black pepper to taste

1. Place a large, heavy-bottomed pot over medium heat.

2. Add the oil, onion, carrots, and celery. Cook until the onion and celery are translucent, stirring occasionally.

3. Add the chili flakes, if using them.

4. Turn the heat up just a bit and add the butternut squash, adding a touch more oil if necessary.

5. Mix well and add the cumin, paprika, and salt. Cook until the butternut squash has developed a deep color, stirring occasionally to prevent the squash from sticking to the pot.

6. Add enough water to cover the squash, then stir in the liquid smoke and simmer until the squash has cooked through completely, poking it with a fork occasionally to check if it's tender.

7. Using an immersion blender, puree the soup completely. Alternatively, you can pour the soup into a stand blender, puree it, adding stock or water as necessary, and move it back to the pot.

8. Add the kale and lemon juice, then turn the heat back on low and simmer, covered, until the kale is soft, about 10 to 15 minutes.

9. Season with pepper and serve immediately.

KID-FRIENDLY TIP: Cutting the kale into thinner strips or pieces will make it a bit easier for little mouths. You can also blanch the kale before cooking it in the pot to make it even more tender.

smoky white bean & black rice soup with kale chips

SERVES 4

This dish is a big bowl of health! I'll be honest, though—I probably wouldn't have gone anywhere near it as a kid. In fact, I would've told my mom she was crazy if she tried to feed this soup to me. As I've mentioned, though—holy wow, was I a picky child. I guess what I'm saying is, the kid-friendliness of this meal will be determined by your child's current food interests, although I have included some tips at the end to help amp up the kid-appeal factor. I'm lucky that Marlowe is a big fan of kale and smoky, tomatoey things, so we all enjoy this together at our house.

1 tablespoon olive oil

1 medium onion, small diced

1 celery stalk, finely diced

1 cup (100 g) small-diced baby bell or white mushrooms—or whatever kind you have on hand!

4 to 5 garlic cloves, crushed

½ bunch kale, stems removed and leaves ripped into pieces

A few sprigs of fresh thyme and rosemary

½ teaspoon chili powder

½ teaspoon sweet smoked Spanish paprika

1 teaspoon salt

Black pepper to taste

1 cup (180 g) diced tomatoes (canned, with liquid, is fine!)

4 cups (950 ml) Vegetable Stock (page 116)

One 15-ounce (425 g) can white beans

½ cup (105 g) cooked black rice*

Kale Chips for garnish (recipe follows)

Black rice isn't a very common pantry item, but it's nice to have around for certain meals. I didn't grow up with it in my own household, but my best friend's Nepali mother would make it occasionally, and it boggled my mind each time! My family grew up eating white rice every single day, so I thought black rice was some sort of delicious magic. It turns out that it is sort of like magic—it's packed with nutrients and is really good for you. It truly is a super-food. This meal tastes great any time, but I especially recommend it for cold days or when you feel your immune system growing weak. Your body will thank you.

1. Heat the oil in a large pot over medium heat.

2. Sauté the onion and celery until translucent.

3. Turn the heat up to medium-high and add the mushrooms and garlic. Cook until the mushrooms are slightly brown.

4. Add the kale, herbs, and a splash of water, and cook until the kale begins to wilt.

5. Mix in the spices, salt, pepper, and tomatoes and simmer for another minute.

6. Add the stock and beans and simmer on low for 15 minutes.

7. Remove from the heat and mix in the cooked black rice.

8. Serve garnished with Kale Chips, and feel warm and healthy.

KID-FRIENDLY TIP: If you have yourself a little one who's a bit picky with brothy soups and stews, consider reserving an extra cup of rice. Use a slotted spoon to scoop up some of the beans, kale, and other veggies from the soup and toss them with the black rice to create a kid-friendly rice bowl.

kale chips

SERVES 4

½ bunch kale, stems removed and leaves torn into bite-size pieces
Drizzle of olive oil
Splash of apple cider vinegar
Salt and nutritional yeast to taste

1. Preheat the oven to 400°F (200°C).

2. Toss the kale in oil and vinegar and place on a baking sheet.

3. Bake for about 10 to 15 minutes, until the kale chips are crispy and beginning to brown.

4. Remove from the oven and sprinkle with salt and nutritional yeast.

yuca & plantain stew

Depending on your location, you might be scratching your head at this dish, as I'm not sure how easy it is to find plantains and yuca in supermarkets around the country (they're everywhere in South Florida). I think you can find just about any ingredient these days, though, no matter where you are; I suggest trying international markets if your local grocery store doesn't carry these. When you want to fill your kitchen and your stomach with a tropical vibe and can easily grab some plantains and yuca, then try this stew. It's sweet, savory, and especially good if you add some extra-spicy chile peppers to it!

1½ tablespoons olive oil or coconut oil

1 medium onion, chopped

1 large celery stalk, diced

¾ cup (130 g) chopped bell pepper

1 teaspoon liquid smoke

½ teaspoon coriander

1 teaspoon spicy smoked Spanish paprika

2 teaspoons salt

4 cups (950 ml) Vegetable Stock (see page 116)

3 cups (624 g) peeled and chopped yuca

1 cup (150 g) peeled and chopped sweet potato or other root vegetable (I suggest boniato [white sweet potato] or malanga [taro])

3 garlic cloves, minced or pressed

1 ripe plantain, peeled and cubed

1 teaspoon white wine vinegar

1. Heat the oil in a large pot over medium heat.

2. Add the onion, celery, and pepper and cook until the onion and celery are translucent.

3. Mix in the liquid smoke, spices, and salt and stir for a few seconds to blend the flavors.

4. Add the stock, yuca, sweet potato, and garlic and simmer for a few minutes until the vegetables begin to soften.

5. Mix in the plantain and cook for another minute, until the root vegetables are soft and the plantain has absorbed the stock.

6. Add the vinegar and simmer for another minute before serving.

KID-FRIENDLY TIP: I've found that this recipe can be hit-or-miss with little ones. It's on the sweeter side because of the sweet potato and ripe plantain, which appeals to a lot of kids (and grown-ups, too, of course)—but Marlowe's least favorite vegetables are sweet potatoes and peppers, and since this soup has both . . . well, it doesn't go over as smoothly as some of the other soups in this home.

TIP FOR LEFTOVERS: Simmer or strain out any extra broth and serve the remaining mixture in a burrito with black beans, rice, and all your favorite toppings. This is absolutely wonderful for breakfast, lunch, or dinner.

TIP: This recipe really sits somewhere between a stew and a soup; it works incredibly well as either. Simmer it down for something chunkier, or keep more stock to have a lighter (but still very filling) dish. Pair it with rice or top it with avocado and—*boom*—you've got a filling, well-rounded meal.

vegetable & bean chili

SERVES 4

began my adventures in cooking with slow-cooker chili. I haven't used a slow-cooker in ages, but it served me very well when I was first learning how to properly feed myself while working morning-to-late-night shifts. I'd be able to toss everything into it in the morning and come home to a finished meal. Now that I know the kitchen basics, I find it just as easy to make a big (non-slow-cooker) batch of chili to eat and reheat as necessary. The ingredient list for this recipe is no different than the one from my early days of learning how to cook, and it's not that much harder, either. The big difference lies in the depth of flavor you achieve by taking a few extra minutes to sauté your vegetables and really meld your flavors together. Slow-cookers can make good stews, soups, and chilies, but adding that special layer of care to the vegetables creates great ones.

1 to 2 tablespoons olive oil

1 small onion, diced

¾ cup (130 g) chopped bell pepper

1 small celery stalk, small diced

1 carrot, diced

⅛ teaspoon chipotle

¼ teaspoon sweet smoked paprika

1 teaspoon chili powder

1 teaspoon salt, divided

1 small zucchini or yellow squash, diced

4 garlic cloves, minced

1 cup (180 g) chopped tomatoes (fresh or canned; I almost always go for canned, but I'm happy to use fresh when available)

1 tablespoon tomato paste

One 15-ounce (425 g) can pinto beans, not drained

One 15-ounce (425 g) can kidney beans, not drained

Vegetable Stock (page 116) or water

½ to 1 tablespoon cocoa powder

Black pepper to taste

Cilantro or avocado with lime for garnish

1. Coat the bottom of a large pot with olive oil and place over medium-high heat.

2. Sauté the onion, pepper, celery, and carrot until the onion is translucent, about 8 minutes.

3. Add the spices, ½ teaspoon salt, and zucchini and sauté for another 3 minutes or so.

4. Mix in the garlic and tomatoes and sauté for another minute.

5. Add the tomato paste, blending it in with the other ingredients.

6. Stir in the beans, with the liquid from the cans, and enough water or vegetable stock to cover your beans and vegetables.

7. Mix in the cocoa powder, then add ½ teaspoon salt and season with pepper.

8. Simmer for about 10 minutes, or until it reaches your desired thickness.

9. Garnish with fresh cilantro or avocado and a squirt of lime and serve with Plantain Corn Bread (page 262).

TIP FOR LEFTOVERS: Reduce any extra liquid down to almost nothing and serve the leftovers as a variation on Lentil Sloppy Joes (page 70). This would also be great served over rice. You can also try adding it to a burrito with avocado or to a baked sweet potato.

A NOTE ABOUT THIS RECIPE

After many years as a bad vegetarian, when I decided to become a vegan, I discovered I really had to start from scratch—slowly teaching myself how to cook, what to cook, what spices to use, and, well, everything. Most vegetables and spices were a whole new game for me. I started with a basic: chili. Making chili, or any stew, is pretty simple. In fact, I think it's hard to make a bad stew. And it's easy to make a decent one. A great stew . . . well, that takes a little bit of knowledge. Not a lot, though—just a bit; it's still one of the basics, after all.

shepherd's pie

This dish, above all others, gets me super-emotional, since it's something my paternal grandmother often fixed for me. She made a super-easy pie with just corn and mashed potatoes—and beef, of course. Nothing more and nothing less. Out of love for me, she offered to feed it to me long past the point that I stopped eating meat. She knew that at one point in time, this was her go-to recipe that was guaranteed to please me, so she insisted on making it despite my switch to vegetarianism. For me, this is the height of comfort food—love in a savory pie. My recipe is rather different than my grandmother's. Number one: it doesn't have beef in it. Number two: I'm actually not sure whether my grandmother used real or instant potatoes! And number three: my recipe is packed with lots of veggies and flavors, but it's still approachable for kids and picky eaters. One trick that I learned from my grandmother, and still use to this day, is to serve this with a bit of fancy homemade Ketchup (page 252). It might not be very traditional (although, let's be honest, neither is using lentils instead of beef), but that's the way she did it, and it makes me just as happy now as it did back then.

1½ tablespoons olive oil

1 medium onion, small diced

1 large carrot, small diced

1 celery stalk, small diced

½ cup (50 g) small-diced mushrooms (your favorite kind)

½ cup (62 g) small-diced zucchini

1 teaspoon salt, or to taste

2 to 3 garlic cloves, minced + 1 clove, pressed

A few sprigs of fresh thyme

2 teaspoons minced fresh rosemary, or to taste

1 teaspoon dried oregano

¾ cup (185 ml) red wine

1 cup (200 g) dried green lentils

2½ cups (600 ml) Vegetable Stock (page 116)

1 to 1½ tablespoons red wine vinegar

Black pepper to taste

1½ cups (240 g) fresh, frozen, or canned (and drained) corn

3 cups (750 g) mashed potatoes

1. Heat the olive oil in a large pan or pot over medium heat.

2. Sauté the onion, carrot, and celery for 3 to 5 minutes.

3. Add the mushrooms and zucchini and sauté until the mushrooms are well cooked and the onion is translucent. Sprinkle in the salt.

4. Mix in the garlic, thyme, rosemary, oregano, and red wine and simmer for 1 minute.

5. Add the lentils and vegetable stock. Simmer for about 25 minutes, until the lentils are well cooked, adding additional stock as needed.

6. Finish with the red wine vinegar, pepper, and another pinch of rosemary, if desired.

7. Preheat the oven to 375°F (190°C).

8. Spread the lentil mixture across the bottom of an oven-safe casserole dish.

9. Sprinkle an even layer of corn across the lentil mixture, then carefully smooth mashed potatoes across the top.

10. Cover and cook for 30 minutes, until heated through (you should be able to see a bit of the liquid lightly simmering).

KID-FRIENDLY TIP: Want to add an extra vegetable to your kid's meal? Use Eggplant Mashed Potatoes (page 112) in place of regular mashed potatoes.

chickpea pot pie

SERVES 4

'I've had some of the most unexpected people (i.e., meat-lovers) tell me how much they adore this. Pot pie is one of those dishes that will always be associated with meat, but when you try this version, you won't feel as if you're missing out on anything. And since it's packed with a healthy amount of vegetables, you won't feel as bad chowing down on some flaky piecrust. You can easily make one giant pie, but I prefer making individual servings, since it means fewer fights over who has more piecrust. I should confess that I used chickpeas in this recipe not only because I have an obsession with them, but because the wordplay that came with them was just too tempting. Luckily, despite the similarity in names, there's no chicken in this, and there doesn't need to be, because it's a really damn good pie without it.

2 tablespoons dairy-free butter

1 medium onion, diced

1 celery stalk, diced

½ cup (75 g) chopped green beans (bite-size pieces)

2 garlic cloves, minced

2 tablespoons minced fresh oregano and thyme

2 heaping tablespoons all-purpose flour

1 cup (250 ml) Vegetable Stock (page 116) or water

2 teaspoons salt

1 cup (250 g) chopped potatoes (bite-size pieces)

1 cup (128 g) chopped carrots (bite-size pieces)

One 15-ounce (425 g) can chickpeas, not drained*

1½ cups (350 ml) dairy-free milk

¼ cup (40 g) fresh, frozen, or canned (and drained) corn

¼ cup (35 g) fresh, frozen, or canned (and drained) peas

¼ cup (15 g) chopped chives

Piecrust (page 268), stored in the fridge until needed

1. Preheat the oven to 375°F (190°C).

2. Melt the butter in a large pot over medium heat. Add the onion and celery and sauté until translucent.

3. Mix in the green beans and garlic and sauté for another 3 minutes or so, until the beans are bright green.

4. Stir in the oregano and thyme, then add the flour, coating the vegetables with it.

5. Pour the stock into the pot a little at a time, stirring to incorporate everything well, especially the flour.

6. Mix in the salt, potatoes, and carrots. Simmer until the potatoes begin to soften, 5 to 7 minutes.

7. Add the chickpeas and milk. Give the mixture a good stir and allow it to simmer for another minute.

8. Remove from the heat, then add the corn, peas, and chives and mix well. Pour the mixture into a 9-inch (23 cm) pie pan, or four individual-size, oven-safe dishes.

9. Roll the pie dough out on a floured surface and cut it to fit the shape of the dish(es), with a little lip left over. Carefully place the dough on top and seal the edges. Cut a few slits to allow steam to escape.

10. Place the dish(es) on a large baking sheet (in case of spillage) and cook for 35 to 45 minutes, until the crust is nice and golden!

White beans also work wonderfully in this recipe.

TIP: Make this all the time.

TIP FOR LEFTOVERS: Not that there will be leftovers, but this freezes pretty well when made in individual servings. To defrost, pull the covered dish out of the freezer and place it in the fridge the morning or night before you want to eat it, then reheat it in a 350°F (175°C) oven until the inside is hot, 5 to 10 minutes.

A NOTE ABOUT THIS RECIPE

I'm the only person I know who truly enjoys a big bowl of pot pie in the summer. Sure, it might be more ideal—romantic, even—to have it on a chilly winter evening, but for me, there's something special about eating pot pie when it's warm outside.

white bean stew with herbed biscuits

SERVES 4

You might be able to guess a few things that I love in my cooking. Vegetables, obviously. Comfort food, of course. But herbs, too—I really can't say enough about them. I mean, not only are they good for you, but they add so much flavor to a meal. This delightful stew really packs in the herbs—and so do the biscuits. Warming, hearty, and truly good for you, this is a winning feast in itself.

WHITE BEAN STEW

1 tablespoon olive oil

1 medium onion, diced

1 celery stalk, small diced

1 cup (100 g) diced white or baby bello mushrooms

1½ cups (90 g) chopped fresh herbs (basil, thyme, oregano, parsley)

3 garlic cloves, chopped or sliced

2 tablespoons all-purpose flour

2 to 2½ cups (500 to 600 ml) Vegetable Stock (page 116)

2 carrots, chopped

2 small to medium creamer potatoes, chopped

1 teaspoon white wine vinegar

1½ teaspoons salt, or to taste

1 tablespoon nutritional yeast

One 15-ounce (425 g) can white beans, not drained

1¼ cups (175 g) fresh, frozen, or canned (and drained) peas

Black pepper to taste

HERBED BISCUITS

Biscuit dough (page 266)

½ cup (30 g) chopped fresh herbs (rosemary, thyme, oregano, basil)

1. Preheat the oven to 400°F (200°C).

2. Heat the oil in a large oven-safe pot over medium heat.

3. Add the onion, celery, and mushrooms and cook until the onion and celery are translucent.

Recipe continues...

4. Mix in the herbs and garlic and sauté for another 30 seconds.

5. Whisk in the flour to create a roux.

6. Slowly add the vegetable stock, whisking continuously to loosen and mix in the flour. Continue until all the stock has been added.

7. Add the carrots, potatoes, white wine vinegar, salt, and nutritional yeast. Mix it all together and simmer for a few minutes, until the carrots and potatoes begin to soften.

8. Mix in the beans (with the liquid), and simmer for another minute. The stew should be thick and hearty—if the stew is too brothy, your vegetables will sink!

9. Remove from the heat and mix in the peas, then season with salt and pepper.

10. Pull your biscuit dough out of fridge, or make a fresh batch now. To make the herbed biscuits, place your ball of dough on a floured surface and sprinkle half the herbs on top. Knead until the herbs begin to stick, then add the remaining herbs and continue to knead for another 2 minutes.

11. Roll the dough out and cut it into 2- to 3-inch (5 to 8 cm) biscuits, or simply pull off golf ball–size sections of dough. Gently place the pieces of dough in the pot on top of the stew.

12. Place the whole dish in the oven and cook until the biscuits are golden, about 9 to 11 minutes. Serve immediately.

A NOTE ABOUT THIS RECIPE

I receive a lot of emails about cooking and eating a plant-based diet and how that works in relation to other people and social occasions. One of the questions I'm often asked is how I handle attending dinner parties that aren't specifically for vegans. I always recommend bringing a big dish (or two) that's filling, easy to carry, and that you love and know others will, too. This is a great recipe for that, especially for winter holiday events. It's a rather beautiful thing to carry a single large pot into someone's home, pull up the lid, and show off the beautiful, rustic, herbed biscuits sitting on top of a delicious, veggie-based stew. Simply ask the hostess if you can place the pot back in the oven to warm for a few minutes, and serve hot. Anyone would be pleased to find this at their next dinner party. I should make clear, though, that this dish is in no way just for dinner parties—it's actually a very normal, everyday meal for my family. We happily make it for just the three of us on any given day.

easy plant-powered dishes

15-minute vegetable couscous

SERVES 3 TO 4

Subtitle: the really fast meal that you throw together when you want to quickly stuff your face with healthy food. I practically lived off variations of this dish in my first few years of motherhood. In this recipe, I've listed the vegetables and spices that I use most often, but I'll let you in on a secret: you can play around with whatever scraps and bits are in your fridge. This recipe is perfect for that. No zucchini? No problem. Use eggplant or bell peppers instead; really just use whatever you love or have on hand! The trick isn't in the veggies you use—the important things are adding the right amount of spices, cooking your veggies until they're nice and tender, and getting the couscous to the ideal consistency. Make this to fill your belly with delicious food in a very short amount of time, and then get back to work, relaxing, or whatever else you're trying to squeeze into your day.

1 tablespoon + 1½ teaspoons olive oil, divided

1 small onion, diced

1 cup (100 g) diced mushrooms (your favorite variety)

1 cup (124 g) cubed zucchini

2 garlic cloves

¾ teaspoon sweet smoked Spanish paprika

¾ teaspoon cumin

¾ teaspoon coriander

¾ teaspoon dried oregano

⅓ to ½ cup (50 to 75 g) halved cherry tomatoes

1 teaspoon salt, divided

1 cup (164 g) cooked or canned chickpeas

¾ cup (130 g) dried Israeli couscous

1 cup (250 ml) water or stock

1 tablespoon nutritional yeast

Handful of fresh greens

2 tablespoons chopped fresh basil

Sliced avocado to taste (optional)

1. Heat 1 tablespoon of the olive oil in a medium pot over medium heat. Add the onion and mushrooms and cook until the onion is translucent.

2. Mix in the zucchini and garlic and cook for another 2 to 3 minutes, until the zucchini shrinks down and has released some of its liquid. Add the spices and the remaining olive oil and mix.

3. Turn up the heat just a tad and add the cherry tomatoes and ½ teaspoon of salt. After the tomatoes begin to slightly blister, add the chickpeas, couscous, water, and the remaining ½ teaspoon of salt and stir.

4. Bring the water to a boil, then reduce the heat and simmer lightly until almost all the liquid is absorbed and the couscous is cooked through, about 8 minutes. Add the nutritional yeast, greens, fresh basil, and mix everything together.

5. When the liquid has completely evaporated, your quick, healthy meal is ready. Top with slices of avocado or more greens, then plop yourself down to enjoy!

stewed chickpeas & okra

SERVES 2 TO 4

This simple, delicious dish makes it easy to please everyone. You can cook it in minutes, or let it simmer for hours. Plus, it tastes even better the next day! This recipe makes enough for two people as a full meal, or four as a side, but feel free to double or triple it if necessary. Add a dash of cayenne pepper if you crave some heat.

2 tablespoons coconut oil, divided

1 small red onion, diced

1 teaspoon garam masala

½ teaspoon curry powder

1 teaspoon coriander seed

½ teaspoon cumin seed

½ teaspoon cayenne pepper (optional)

½ teaspoon salt, or to taste

1½ cups (150 g) sliced okra

1 tablespoon grated ginger

1 tablespoon grated garlic

One 15-ounce (425 g) can diced tomatoes, with liquid

One 15-ounce (425 g) can chickpeas, drained

Chopped cilantro to taste

Chopped chiles to taste

1. Heat 1 tablespoon of the oil in a medium pot over medium heat. Add the onion and cook until soft and translucent, about 5 minutes.

2. Mix in the spices and salt and cook for another minute.

3. Add the okra slices and coat them with the remaining oil. Fry until they lose their moisture and begin to blacken slightly.

4. Stir in the ginger and garlic and cook for another 30 seconds to 1 minute.

5. Add the tomatoes and mix well. Simmer for about 5 minutes, until the tomatoes begin to brown from the spices.

6. Mix in the chickpeas and simmer for 10 to 25 minutes, until the spices have cooked completely into the chickpeas and the sauce, adding a tablespoon of water at a time as necessary to reach your desired texture.

7. Garnish with cilantro and freshly chopped chiles.

breaded eggplant

MAKES 10 TO 15 PIECES

This recipe is sure to please even the most intense eggplant skeptic. Crispy on the outside and tender (but not chewy!) on the inside, this is an incredibly versatile dish. It can impress a lover on a romantic date night (pass the red wine, please!) or work as the perfect finger food for tiny, picky, toddler hands (cheers to apple juice!). For little ones, slice the eggplant rounds in half before breading. Serve with a salad for a full meal, or as a side to a pasta dish. I sometimes even smother it in Our Go-to Red Sauce (page 242) and make an eggplant parm. No matter how you present it, it's fantastic.

1 large eggplant

Coarse sea salt to taste

Olive oil for baking

1 cup (125 g) all-purpose flour

½ cup (125 ml) almond milk

1½ cups (165 g) dried bread crumbs

½ cup (80 g) nutritional yeast

1 teaspoon finely ground salt

1 tablespoon dried oregano

1 tablespoon dried basil

1. Peel the eggplant and slice it into ½-inch (1.25 cm) thick rounds.

2. Heavily salt the eggplant with the coarse sea salt and let it sit for at least 30 minutes to draw out the excess moisture. After half an hour, there should be liquid on top of the slices. Wipe them dry.

3. Evenly coat the bottom of a baking sheet with olive oil.

4. Fill one medium bowl with flour, another medium bowl with milk, and a third medium bowl with the remaining ingredients (bread crumbs, nutritional yeast, finely ground salt, oregano, and basil).

5. Working with one piece at a time, place the eggplant slices into the flour and coat them well on each side.

6. Place the floured eggplant into the milk, then drop it into the bread-crumb mixture and coat well on each side.

7. Place the eggplant slices on the oiled baking sheet.

8. Repeat the process with each eggplant slice until none remain.

9. Bake for 20 minutes, then flip each slice and bake for another 8 to 10 minutes, until golden. Serve warm.

chickpea patties

Every time we eat these at my house, we all look around at each other and ask, "Why don't we have these more often?!" This was the first veggie burger I made from scratch, and over the years I've tweaked the recipe slightly here and there to make it even better. They're absolutely perfect on a bun, but we love them most served on a nice bed of mixed greens and fresh veggies, with Sherry Vinaigrette (page 241) drizzled on top. Add a glass of lemonade, and you have an ideal meal for a warm, breezy day.

One 15-ounce (425 g) can chickpeas, drained

2 garlic cloves

⅓ cup (53 g) fresh or frozen corn

½ cup (70 g) fresh or frozen and thawed peas

Large handful of fresh herbs (I like to use basil, oregano, and/or thyme)

One to two large handfuls of spinach (optional)

2 medium carrots, shredded

1 small onion, small diced

½ teaspoon spicy smoked Spanish paprika (optional)

½ teaspoon cumin (optional)

3 tablespoons dried bread crumbs

3 tablespoons all-purpose flour

Salt and black pepper to taste

Olive oil for cooking

1. In a food processor, blend together the chickpeas, garlic, corn, peas, herbs, and spinach (if using) for a few minutes, until smooth.

2. Add the carrots, onion, spices, bread crumbs, and flour to the food processor and blend together. Turn out the mixture into a large bowl and season with salt and pepper.

3. Heat the oil in a skillet over medium-high heat.

4. Form the mixture into patties (we like to make 3½-inch [9 cm] patties) and fry until golden, 3 to 5 minutes per side. You can cook a few at a time, but keep in mind that they're much easier to flip when you have more space! Do not fuss with the burgers while they're cooking; flip them just once, very carefully.

TIP: These are great for freezing—you'll never need to buy a processed veggie burger again! Once the patties have fully cooled, individually wrap each one and place in a freezer-safe container in the freezer for later. When you're ready to enjoy them again, reheat on the stove in an oiled pan or in the oven on low heat until heated through.

hearts of palm patties

MAKES 6 LARGE PATTIES

Be warned: You might need a nap after eating these veggie patties! They taste richly indulgent and satisfying, but never fear, hearts of palm are actually low in fat and a good source of protein and other vitamins. An absolutely perfect scenario for me would involve these, sunshine, and a hammock to lie in after devouring one. I ate many of these throughout my pregnancy, and even now they always hit the spot. They're great for a family lunch, or made into bite-size slider versions for parties. Your taste buds will thank me.

Olive oil for cooking

½ cup (80 g) diced onion

½ cup (90 g) diced bell pepper

One 14- to 15-ounce (400 to 425 g) can hearts of palm, drained

1 garlic clove

¼ cup (60 g) vegan mayo

1 teaspoon Dijon mustard

5 tablespoons dried bread crumbs

Zest of 1 lemon

1 tablespoon diced fresh parsley

1 tablespoon diced fresh cilantro

Salt and black pepper to taste

Buns for serving (optional)

1. Heat about 1 tablespoon of the oil in a skillet over medium heat. Add the onion and pepper and sauté until translucent, about 5 minutes.

2. Blend the hearts of palm and garlic together in a food processor. Turn the mixture out into a large bowl, and add the remaining ingredients (except the buns, of course). Combine thoroughly, seasoning with salt and pepper as necessary.

3. Form into 3-inch (8 cm) patties (or whatever size best fits your buns).

4. Coat the skillet with some additional oil and heat it over medium-high heat. Fry the patties until golden, 3 to 5 minutes per side. Do not fuss with the burgers while they're cooking; flip them just once, very carefully.

"nacho" baked potato

This recipe makes a great go-to meal for busy parents or new moms. It's super-quick, super-easy, super-filling, and even has some nutritional value to it! All you need is a few minutes during your kid's nap time, and—*boom!* You have a real meal to enjoy, and it didn't come out of a box. I recommend baking a bunch of potatoes in advance to have them handy for the rest of the week, or you can simply "bake" the potato in the microwave right beforehand. In my opinion, this is already so perfect that it doesn't need cheese, but it's delicious with it, too, if that's your preference. You can make your own black beans and salsa, use leftovers, or even just use store-bought brands in a pinch. I do, of course, recommend spending the extra five minutes to make salsa—but I promise I won't judge you if you don't.

1 large baking potato

Olive oil to taste

1½ teaspoons nutritional yeast (optional)

½ cup (113 g) black beans, either canned or prepared as directed for Black Beans (page 176), heated through

¼ cup (57 g) Salsa de Molcajete (page 186), or salsa of your choice

¼ to ½ avocado, cubed, sliced, or smashed

Salt and black pepper to taste

Cilantro for garnish

Lime wedges for garnish

1. Preheat the oven to 450°F (230°C) if baking the potato (rather than microwaving it).

2. Pierce the potato with a fork or knife a few times to allow the steam to escape. Bake in the oven for about 40 minutes, or microwave for 4 to 6 minutes, depending on the size of the potato. Pierce the potato with a fork or knife to check if it is soft and cooked through.

3. When the potato is done, slice it open, drizzle some of the olive oil on top, and sprinkle on the nutritional yeast, if using.

4. Layer on the black beans, salsa, and avocado. Drizzle some more olive oil on top, then season with salt and pepper. Garnish with cilantro and lime.

5. Eat your yummy, healthy meal full of protein, good fat, and vegetables.

black bean burgers

MAKES 4 TO 6 BURGERS

This is quite possibly the easiest veggie burger known to man. In about 15 minutes you can have yummy black bean burgers to feed your whole family. Try the burgers by themselves with just your favorite toppings, or serve them with a side of rice, chips, or plantains. We eat ours on buns—sometimes even with Ketchup (page 252)—but they're also great on a salad with sliced avocado!

Two 14-ounce (400 g) cans black beans, drained

Small handful of fresh cilantro and oregano

1 garlic clove

1½ teaspoons lime juice

1 teaspoon spicy smoked Spanish paprika

1 teaspoon cumin

½ cup (80 g) diced onion

2 tablespoons all-purpose flour

Salt and black pepper to taste

Olive oil for the pan

Buns for serving (optional)

TOPPING SUGGESTIONS:

Sliced avocado

Cilantro

Guacamole

Salsa de Molcajete (page 186)

Green Tomatillo Hot Sauce (page 188)

Mango Cilantro Sauce (page 247)

1. Blend the black beans, fresh herbs, garlic, lime juice, paprika, and cumin in a food processor until smooth.

2. Combine the mixture with the onion and flour in a large bowl. Season with salt and pepper.

3. Using your hands, form the mixture into round 3-inch (8 cm) patties, or whatever size best fits your buns.

4. Cook in a well-oiled skillet over medium-high heat for 3 to 5 minutes on each side, until the patties are slightly browned. Do not fuss with them; flip them just once, very carefully.

5. Serve immediately with your desired toppings and sides.

latin american favorites

baked plantains

Okay, I admit it . . . we typically fry our plantains. But we're trying to promote some new, healthier habits, right? Right. This recipe is an absolutely delicious way to do so—it practically turns the plantains into dessert. Eat these on toast (one of our favorite ways to enjoy them; see page 61), with Rice & Beans (page 162), with Black Beans (page 176), as a side for brunch, or however else your heart desires—the possibilities are endless.

3 very ripe (black) plantains

1 to 2 tablespoons coconut oil*

1. Preheat the oven to 450°F (230°C).

2. Cut the tips off the plantains, then slice the peel all the way down the length of the plantain and remove the peel.

3. Thinly slice the plantains to about ¼- to ½-inch (6 to 12 mm) thick and coat the slices with the coconut oil.

4. Spread the plantains in a single layer on a baking sheet and bake for 10 to 15 minutes, gently flipping them once halfway through cooking. They should be golden, slightly burnt, and delicious.

*This recipe calls for coconut oil, but canola oil will work, too.

TIP: Interested in frying your plantains? Fill a large pot or pan with 1 to 2 inches (2.5 to 5 cm) of coconut oil, canola oil, or a mixture of both and place over medium-high heat. Once the oil is hot, carefully slide each plantain slice in one at a time and fry until golden brown. Place the cooked pieces on a paper towel to soak up the extra oil before serving.

rice & beans

SERVES 4

Ask my daughter, "What's your favorite food?" and almost every time her response is "rice and beans and tofu." Although there's no tofu in this dish, the rice and beans are here—with lots of staple veggies, too. This is a perfect one-pot meal: it's inexpensive, filling, incredibly easy to make, and packed with vegetables and protein. I love to eat it with hot sauce, and everyone in my family enjoys it topped with avocado and lime. The day is made extra-bright when we have a fried (or baked!) plantain to pair with the meal.

1½ tablespoons olive oil

1 medium onion, small diced

½ cup (90 g) diced pepper, any variety—choose your favorite, or stick to a poblano or bell pepper

¾ cup (75 g) diced baby bella or white button mushrooms

1½ teaspoons cumin

1½ teaspoons sweet smoked Spanish paprika

½ teaspoon chili powder

1 tablespoon dried oregano

1 teaspoon salt

4 garlic cloves, sliced

1 cup (180 g) chopped tomatoes (we use fresh, but canned is fine, too)

One 15-ounce (425 g) can black beans, drained but not rinsed

1 cup (185 g) uncooked white rice

About 1½ cups (350 ml) water or Vegetable Stock (page 116); refer to the cooking directions on the rice package for exact amount

Chopped cilantro for garnish

Lime slices or wedges for garnish

1. Heat the oil in a large pot over medium heat. Make sure the oil coats the entire bottom of the pan.

2. Add the onion, pepper, and mushrooms and sauté until soft and cooked down.

3. Stir in the spices and salt and mix well.

4. Add the garlic and tomatoes and cook for 1 to 2 minutes, until very little moisture remains.

5. Mix in the beans, rice, and water or stock and bring to a boil.

6. Once the mixture is boiling, cover the pot with a lid and lower the heat to the lowest setting. Cook for 20 minutes, or as directed on rice package.

7. Turn off the heat, but leave the pot covered for another 10 minutes to allow the rice to continue to steam.

8. When it's time, remove the lid and fluff the rice and beans with a fork.

9. Garnish with cilantro and lime. Serve with avocados, fried plantains, and your favorite hot sauce.

THE PLANTIFUL TABLE

chile-braised pinto beans

SERVES 4

Alex and I are similar in numerous ways and different in many others. Beans are one thing that separates us. I believe black beans are superior, while he thinks pinto beans rule all. Here's the thing—both are good. And this recipe, which is his, tastes spectacular. That said, it requires a bit more time than a lot of busy parents can manage on an average day. I try to keep that in mind when creating recipes, because I know our lives are fast-paced, even when we intentionally try to spend more time in the kitchen. So maybe you won't make this recipe every night, but on the weekends or days that allow more time for cooking, do try it. Everyone will love this slow-cooked, flavor-packed dish that makes pinto beans king.

1. Heat the olive oil and achiote in a large heavy-bottomed pot or Dutch oven over medium heat.

2. Add the chiles and toast them for a minute, then add the onion and cook for 10 minutes.

3. Season with 1 teaspoon of salt. Add the garlic and continue cooking for another 5 minutes.

4. Mix in the bay leaves, oregano, and cumin. Toast for 1 minute.

5. Add the beans and water and season with the remaining salt and the black pepper.

6. Bring to a boil, then cover with a lid and simmer for 1 hour.

7. At the last minute, stir in the brown sugar and sherry vinegar.

8. Serve these as a side dish, or spoon some into a Tortilla (page 264) with rice and Green Tomatillo Hot Sauce (page 188) for a yummy taco or burrito.

This tropical red spice can usually be found in Hispanic markets or the ethnic-foods aisle in grocery stores. If you can't find it, though, feel free to skip it!

1 tablespoon olive oil

1 teaspoon ground achiote (ground annatto)*

3 California chiles, stemmed and seeded

1 large onion, diced

3 teaspoons salt, divided

4 garlic cloves

3 bay leaves

2 teaspoons dried oregano

1 teaspoon ground cumin

Two 15-ounce (425 g) cans pinto beans

½ cup (125 ml) water

Freshly cracked black pepper to taste

1 teaspoon brown sugar

1 teaspoon sherry vinegar

paella

SERVES ABOUT 6

aella is one of the first meals that my mom officially "vegan-ized" for me. Although it had a few questionable ingredients (such as yellow food coloring), it was good (really good— Mom, I love you). But, as with all things in life, there's always room for improvement, so I created this clean, simple, and beautiful version of the classic rice dish. My mother would be so proud (Alex's paella-loving grandmother, too). Marlowe? Well, she likes it overall but hates those pesky peppers. This is full of flavors and textures, and cooking it makes the whole house smell like home to me—and maybe to you, too, if you grew up in a Hispanic household. By the way, this recipe makes a lot. It's intended feed your entire family, Hispanic or not.

4 cups (950 ml) Vegetable Stock (page 116)

10 saffron threads

3 tablespoons olive oil

1 medium onion, diced

1 red bell pepper, diced

3 teaspoons salt, divided

Freshly cracked black pepper to taste

4 garlic cloves, sliced

1 cup (180 g) fresh or canned chopped tomatoes

2 teaspoons spicy smoked Spanish paprika

2 cups (370 g) medium-grain Valencia rice

1 cup (250 ml) dry white wine

One 15-ounce (425 g) can chickpeas, drained

Two 14-ounce (400 g) cans quartered artichoke hearts, drained

1 cup (110 g) chopped fresh green beans

½ cup (70 g) fresh or frozen peas

Roasted red peppers for garnish

Parsley for garnish

1. Heat the vegetable stock in a medium pot over high heat.

2. Once the stock is boiling, remove the pot from the heat and add the saffron. Set aside to allow the saffron threads to bloom until the broth is needed.

3. Preheat the oven to 400°F (200°C).

4. Heat the olive oil in a heavy-bottomed Dutch oven or paella pan over medium-low heat.

Recipe continues...

5. Add the onion, pepper, and 1 teaspoon of salt, then season with black pepper. Slowly sweat the vegetables for 8 to 10 minutes, allowing the moisture to cook out without browning the vegetables.

6. Mix in the garlic and cook for another 5 minutes.

7. Stir in the tomatoes and another teaspoon of salt and cook for a few more minutes.

8. Add the paprika and toast for about 2 minutes, until very fragrant.

9. Mix in the rice and lightly toast for 2 minutes, stirring frequently to ensure all the rice grains get some action.

10. Deglaze the pan with white wine and reduce the mixture until almost all the liquid is gone.

11. Stir in the stock, chickpeas, artichokes, green beans, peas, and the last teaspoon of salt. Raise the heat to medium-high.

12. Continue cooking for a few more minutes, stirring frequently, until the mixture is simmering and the rice begins to absorb the broth.

13. When there's just enough liquid in the pot to completely cover the rice, put the whole pot, uncovered, in the oven for 15 to 20 minutes.

14. If you want to make this really special, after removing it from the oven, place the pot back on the stove over medium heat for a few minutes. This creates a nice, crispy crust on the bottom of the pot.

15. Garnish with fresh roasted peppers and parsley. *Boom*—you now have a Hispanic-mother-approved meal!

TIP FOR LEFTOVERS: Share with friends!

tamales

MAKES 20 TAMALES

Try these if you want to impress your friends and family and fill their bellies with an authentic vegan tamale. Although the recipe requires a bit of prep and cook time, if you prepare the tamales in large batches, they're perfect for dinner parties and freezing for future meals. We like to serve them to our friends with an array of salsas and beans (black bean and/ or pinto) to use as toppings. This is also great with the Red Mole Sauce (page 172). It dials your typical taco dinner up a notch. There may be a lot of steps involved, but, thankfully, they're easy ones—so go ahead and pour yourself a tequila cocktail while you cook.

1. Soak the corn husks in a bowl of water.

2. Heat the olive oil in a medium or large pot over medium heat.

3. Add the carrot and sauté for 3 to 5 minutes.

4. Stir in the onion and pepper and sauté until translucent.

5. Add the corn, garlic, and herbs and sauté for another 2 to 3 minutes, until the corn develops a bright color.

6. Mix in the zucchini, 1 teaspoon of salt, and cumin and cook until the zucchini is tender. Remove from the heat and set aside while you make your tamale dough.

7. Combine the flour, 1½ teaspoons of salt, and baking powder in a large bowl. Mix well.

8. Pour in the water, stirring until well blended.

9. Add the shortening and combine everything thoroughly, then add the cooked veggies and mix. Your filling is ready!

Recipe continues...

20 corn husks

1 tablespoon olive oil

1 carrot, small diced

1 small to medium onion, small diced

1 red bell pepper, small diced

1 cup (160 g) fresh or frozen corn

3 garlic cloves, sliced or minced

1 teaspoon chopped thyme

2 teaspoons minced oregano

1 medium zucchini, small diced

2½ teaspoons salt, divided

½ teaspoon cumin

2 cups (250 g) Maseca tamale flour

1 teaspoon baking powder

2 cups (500 ml) water

⅔ cup (150 g) vegetable shortening

Cilantro for garnish

THE PLANTIFUL TABLE

10. Take one corn husk at a time and lay it flat on your work surface. Place a scoop of the tamale filling into the corn-husk wrapper. The amount of filling will depend on the size of your husk, which can vary widely, so play around with it until you figure out what works.

11. Pull the shorter ends over to cover the filling, then, one at a time, wrap the longer ends around the filling. Be sure to wrap tightly so none of the filling spills out. Place the tamales in a large pot seam side down.

12. Steam your tamales for 1 hour.*

13. Serve the tamales while they're hot. Garnish with cilantro and Red Mole (page 172), or any assortment of salsas, sauces, and beans!

*We use a large bamboo steamer that we bought from the Asian market, but a double boiler on the stove works just as well.

KID-FRIENDLY TIP: The kids don't need the tequila if they're helping you make these.

TIP FOR LEFTOVERS: These are ideal snacks for between-meal cravings—just wrap them in plastic or aluminum foil to freeze them individually, then defrost on the counter or in the microwave when you want one. (Unfortunately, they don't last very long in the fridge, since they dry out a bit.) You can re-steam them wrapped in a damp cloth or paper towel to bring back some of the moisture.

red mole

Alex and I created this recipe with the Tamales (page 169) in mind, although it goes great with tacos, too! Don't be scared by the number of ingredients involved—despite the long list, most items should already be in your pantry or are pretty easy to find in a supermarket or health food store. It is a longer and more intensive recipe than some, but the actual steps themselves aren't that difficult.

4 dried California chiles

2 dried ancho chiles

2 tablespoons sesame seeds

¼ cup (35 g) pumpkin seeds

¼ cup (35 g) toasted whole almonds

1 cinnamon stick

3 whole cloves

½ teaspoon peppercorns

3 tablespoons cacao nibs

2 tablespoons olive oil

½ teaspoon ground achiote (ground annatto)

1 medium yellow onion, chopped

4 garlic cloves, smashed

1 red apple, peeled, cored, and chopped

3½ teaspoons salt, divided

1 cup (220 g) crushed tomatoes (fresh or canned is fine!)

2½ cups (600 ml) water

1 tablespoon + 1 teaspoon brown sugar

1. Heat a large cast-iron skillet or griddle over medium heat.

2. Add the dried chiles to the skillet or griddle and toast for 20 seconds on each side, or until they become very fragrant, then remove from the pan immediately.

3. In the same pan, toast the sesame and pumpkin seeds, just until they start popping. Remove immediately.

4. Toast the almonds for 1 to 2 minutes, until the oils start to release and smell fragrant, then remove immediately.

5. Next toast the cinnamon, cloves, and peppercorns until fragrant, about 30 seconds. Remove from the pan.

6. Toast the cacao nibs for 1 to 2 minutes, until oily and fragrant. Remove from the heat.

7. Meanwhile, heat a heavy-bottomed pot or Dutch oven over medium heat. Add the olive oil and achiote. Cook until the oil is bright yellow.

8. Mix in the onion and garlic and allow them to sweat in the pot for 15 minutes, or until translucent, stirring frequently.

9. Add the toasted chiles. Cook for 2 minutes.

10. Stir in the apple, then cook for another 5 minutes.

11. Add 2 teaspoons of salt, plus the tomatoes and water. Simmer until the chiles are plump and soft, about 15 minutes.

12. Transfer the mixture to a blender and add the sesame and pumpkin seeds, almonds, peppercorns, cloves, cinnamon, cacao, brown sugar, and remaining salt.

13. Blend on medium to high speed for several minutes, until the mixture is smooth and velvety.

14. Serve with Tamales (page 169), or anything else you want!

KID-FRIENDLY TIP: This should be mild enough for most kids, but, as always, check the heat levels of your chiles first.

really good vegetable tacos

MAKES 8 TO 10 SMALL TACOS

As the name of the recipe implies, this is a really good, vegetable-heavy taco dish. It's also incredibly simple. Although this might not be a meal to convince a meat-eater that vegan tacos are just like meat ones, that's okay, because they're not—they're not supposed to be. And have I mentioned that this is really, really good?

2 tablespoons olive oil, divided

1 medium onion, small diced

½ bell pepper, small diced

One 14-ounce (400 g) package of your favorite mushrooms, small diced

¼ teaspoon salt + extra to taste

1 medium zucchini or yellow squash, small diced

4 garlic cloves, minced

Pinch of dried oregano (about ½ teaspoon)

¼ cup (45 g) chopped tomatoes

Pinch of chili powder

1 teaspoon sweet smoked Spanish paprika

1 tablespoon minced fresh cilantro for garnish

Eight to ten 4-inch (13 cm) Basic Tortillas (page 264)

1. Heat 1½ tablespoons of the oil in a large skillet over medium-high heat.

2. Add the onion, pepper, and mushrooms and cook until the onion is translucent.

3. Mix in ¼ teaspoon of salt and the zucchini or squash. Sauté until tender.

4. Stir in the remaining oil, along with the garlic and oregano, and cook for a minute.

5. Add the tomatoes, chili powder, and paprika. Simmer for another minute or so, until the excess moisture has steamed out.

6. Season with another pinch of salt and the cilantro.

7. Build your taco and enjoy!

VARIATION:

These tacos are also great with the addition of black or pinto beans. The beans aren't necessary, but they do add some protein if you're looking for it. Just add a 14-ounce (400 g) can of drained beans at the same time as the tomatoes and allow the water to cook down as necessary.

KID-FRIENDLY TIP: You probably couldn't have convinced me to eat this as a kid. When I say probably, I mean definitely. I would have laughed if my mom had suggested it. In other words, this isn't a taco meal for picky eaters—kids or adults. However, if you chop everything up super-small, you just may get away with it.

TIP FOR LEFTOVERS: This would be perfect to add to Calentado (page 48), or you can try it as a brunch accompaniment with Everyone's Favorite Breakfast Potatoes (page 30).

black beans

Everyone I know cooks black beans differently. Even I change it up a bit depending on my mood and level of patience. As long as you have the basics down, black beans don't need a whole lot of added flair to make them oh-so-good—the peppers in this recipe are really just a crunchy addition, not a necessity. These tasty beans are simple enough that every kid and adult will love them, making this a fail-proof dish. We enjoy them garnished with sliced avocado and the Salsa de Molcajete (page 186) and/or Green Tomatillo Hot Sauce (page 188). You can also serve them as tacos, if that's more your thing.

1½ tablespoons olive oil

1 medium onion, small diced

1 red bell pepper, small diced

4 garlic cloves, sliced or diced

2 teaspoons salt

3 teaspoons cumin

3 teaspoons minced oregano

½ to 1 teaspoon red wine vinegar

Two 14-ounce (400 g) cans black beans, with liquid

¼ to ½ cup (60 to 125 ml) water or Vegetable Stock (page 116)

Basic Tortillas (page 264)

1. Heat the olive oil in a medium pot over medium heat. Add the onion and bell pepper and cook until the onion is translucent, stirring occasionally.

2. Mix in the garlic, salt, cumin, and oregano, and cook for another minute or so. Stir in a splash of red wine vinegar.

3. Add the beans and water or stock and simmer over medium to medium-low heat for 8 to 10 minutes, until it reaches your desired consistency.*

4. Place a dollop of the bean filling into a tortilla, fold into a burrito, and serve with garnishes of your choice.

*As long as you cook down the pepper and onion in the beginning, there really is no right or wrong amount of time to cook your beans. Taste them along the way and see what texture and consistency you prefer. They can look a bit unappealing when they're broken down after being cooked for a long time, but, man, are they delicious!

KID-FRIENDLY TIP: Feel free to skip the bell pepper.

TIP FOR LEFTOVERS: Puree this filling and spread it onto a tortilla with a bit of salsa and some nutritional yeast, Cashew Cheese (page 204), or other cheese replacement to create a quesadilla. This is an easy go-to meal for Marlowe and me.

A NOTE ABOUT THIS RECIPE
I grew up watching my mom make black beans every day. No matter what else we had for dinner, she would cook a pot of rice and a pot of beans. But I never ate the beans—just the rice. I'm not sure why, or whether she ever tried to feed the beans to me (probably). If they had come in a burrito or taco, though, there's a chance I might have changed my mind. What I do know is that I'm very happy to eat them now, especially in this recipe.

empanadas

Empanadas vary from country to country and even from region to region. Growing up, my Colombian family was mostly exposed to the corn variety. Although Alex didn't really grow up eating them, Cuban empanadas traditionally use flour for the dough. This recipe is more similar to those, except this one uses vegetable shortening rather than the traditional rendered animal fat. One thing I like about this flour version is how simple it is, especially since I try to keep the beginning home cook in mind when creating recipes. If you're not a dough expert (don't worry; I'm not either), it can be tricky using corn flour to form a vegan dough that's easy to work with. It's not impossible, just slightly more difficult than wheat-based flour. Luckily, this recipe is incredibly straightforward—the dough contains only four main ingredients (not counting water and salt). Just give it some love, and you'll come away with some impressively spice-packed vegan empanadas.

DOUGH

4 cups (500 g) all-purpose flour

2 teaspoons baking powder

1 cup (230 g) vegetable shortening

⅔ cup (160 ml) warm water

⅓ cup (80 ml) dairy-free milk

2 teaspoons salt

FILLING

1 tablespoon olive oil

1 onion, finely chopped

1 carrot, finely chopped

4 garlic cloves, minced

1 large creamer potato, finely chopped

1 teaspoon chopped oregano

½ teaspoon ground achiote (ground annatto)

1 teaspoon cumin

1 teaspoon coriander

½ teaspoon cinnamon

2½ teaspoons salt

Freshly cracked black pepper to taste

One 15-ounce (425 g) can small white beans, drained

1 tablespoon tomato paste

1 cup (250 ml) water

¼ head cauliflower, finely chopped

¼ cup (30 g) pine nuts

1 tablespoon brown sugar

1 teaspoon sherry vinegar

2 tablespoons chopped cilantro

Recipe continues...

To Make the Dough

1. In a large bowl, combine the flour and baking powder and mix well. Add clumps of shortening and gently mash them into the flour, working the dough until all the shortening is completely combined.

2. In a medium bowl, combine the water, milk, and salt, and stir until the salt is fully dissolved.

3. Slowly add the wet ingredients to the dough and mix together. Work the dough until a ball forms.

4. Roll the dough out right then, or set aside until the filling is done. (Leaving it on the counter should be fine, unless you live in the tropics, in which case, you might want to refrigerate the dough until ready to use.)

To Make the Filling

1. Heat the olive oil in a large heavy-bottomed pot over medium heat. Cook the onion, carrot, and garlic until soft.

2. Add the potato, oregano, achiote, cumin, coriander, cinnamon, salt, and pepper. Cook until the spices are toasted, about 1 to 2 minutes.

3. Mix in the beans, tomato paste, water, and cauliflower and simmer until the potato is soft.

4. Add the pine nuts, brown sugar, sherry vinegar, and cilantro. Set aside to cool until you're ready to form the empanadas.

To Make the Empanadas

1. Preheat the oven to 350°F (175°C).

2. On a floured surface, roll the dough out to about ⅛- to ¼-inch (3 to 6 mm) thick.

3. Cut out circles that are the size you want your empanadas to be. About 4 to 6 inches (10 to 15 cm) in diameter is a good size, but you can consider making little 3-inch (8 cm) ones for mini appetizers or small hands.

4. Place a few tablespoons of the filling (the amount will depend on the size of the empanada) in the center of the circle and fold one side of the dough over.

5. There are a few ways to do this next step. Some, such as folding and pinching, are trickier, so my favorite method for closing an empanada is to simply press down the sides with a fork. Make sure you remove all the air from the center pocket first, then use a fork to push down around the edges and secure the dough together. Repeat until the dough and/or filling is used up.

6. Place the empanadas about ½ inch (1.25 cm) apart on a baking sheet and bake for 20 to 30 minutes, depending on the size of the empanadas. You can tell they're ready when they're golden and crispy.

KID-FRIENDLY TIP: Make these child-size! What kid doesn't like something she can hold in her hands? Serve with Ketchup (page 252) and you have a winner.

A NOTE ABOUT THIS RECIPE

So, besides the ease-factor, why did I choose to go with a Cuban-style empanada dough rather the Colombian version from my own background? In general, I tend to prefer wheat over corn when cooking. While it's sad to think that something as simple as truly natural corn-on-the-cob is something our children and grandchildren might not experience, big agriculture seems to run the market these days, and organic and non-genetically modified (NGMO) corn products can be difficult to find, even in health food stores. And while we do use our trusty (probably GMO-guilty) Maseca corn flour for a lot of things, I try to avoid using it too much.

THE PLANTIFUL TABLE

my mother's arepas

'm pretty sure I'm not exaggerating when I tell you that a minimum of one hundred arepas are made and consumed in my mother's home over the course of a one-week visit with her. Home simply isn't home without them. Arepas are like the bread or biscuit of the Colombian world. You can create sandwiches with them, serve them alongside meals, or use them as vehicles for toppings—or they can be eaten as is, of course! The options are endless. Arepas can easily be made without cheese, and they often are, but the best ones are crisp, salty, and filled with melted cheesy goodness. We don't use store-bought vegan cheese often, but we do when my mother is around, just for this recipe.

1. Combine the masarepa and 1¼ cups (300 ml) of the water in a large bowl. Mix until well combined, adding up to ¼ cup (60 ml) of additional water if necessary to reach the correct dough consistency. The mixture should be slightly moist and sticky, but there should be no extra liquid.

2. Add the shredded cheese to the dough and mix until well blended.

3. Using your hands, make ½-inch (1.25 cm) thick, 3-inch (8 cm) wide patties.

4. Coat a large skillet or griddle with oil and place over medium-low heat.

5. Cooking just a few arepas at a time and making sure not to crowd the pan, fry them until brown and crispy, about 3 minutes per side. Don't fuss with them while they cook—just wait for them to crisp up and then flip. When they're done, place them on a paper towel to drain the excess oil while you cook the remaining arepas.

6. Serve with avocado, Easy Tofu Scramble (page 24), Hearty Corn & Avocado Salsa (page 29), or enjoy them just as they are!

1 cup (170 g) white masarepa (pre-cooked corn flour)

1¼ to 1½ cups (300 to 350 ml) warm or room temperature water

1½ cups (180 g) shredded dairy-free cheese

Oil for cooking (olive or canola is fine)

sweet & spicy arepas

MAKES 10 TO 12 AREPAS

These ain't my mama's arepas. Really, though—they're not even close. My mom is about white corn, 100 percent of the time. I totally understand that, but at the same time, mixing it up every once in a while is wonderful, too. The white corn arepas in this book (see the previous recipe on page 182) are basically like Colombian breakfast bread and are intended for you to munch on or to top with things, just like toast. This version is a more playful, spicy-sweet combo. You can skip the hot chile peppers if you're making this for kiddos; it's a recipe I created long before I had to worry about young taste buds, and it's spicy. These are great served with Mango Cilantro Sauce (page 247) or another refreshing accompaniment. They're also great with (dairy-free) cheese mixed in, but they don't need it.

Olive oil for cooking

½ small onion, diced
(about ¼ cup [40 g])

1 cup (175 g) diced peppers
(about ½ sweet, ½ spicy)

1 cup (170) g) yellow masarepa
(pre-cooked corn flour)

1 teaspoon salt

2½ tablespoons sugar

1 cup (300 ml) warm or room
temperature water + extra
if needed

1. Heat about a tablespoon of the olive oil in a frying pan over medium heat. Add the onion and peppers and cook until translucent, then set aside to cool.

2. Mix together the masarepa, salt, and sugar in a large bowl.

3. Add ½ cup (125 ml) of the warm water and blend everything well.

4. Mix in another ½ cup (125 ml) of the water and gently knead the mixture into a dough. It should be slightly moist; if necessary, you can add up to another ¼ cup water.

5. Add the peppers and onion to the bowl and incorporate them into the dough.

6. Form the dough into 6 to 8 little patties, depending on the size you want them (we typically make them about 3 inches [8 cm]).

7. In the same pan that you used to cook the onion and peppers, add a generous amount of olive oil and heat over medium-high.

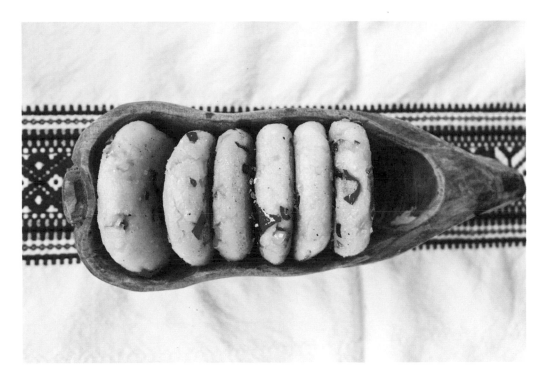

8. Fry the patties in the pan, making sure not to turn them over until the bottom has browned. Gently flip them and fry on other side.

9. Serve with Mango Cilantro Sauce (page 247) or your favorite sweet sauce.

KID-FRIENDLY TIP: When making these to eat with Marlowe, I create a few kid-friendly ones before tossing the spicy chile peppers into the mix. It's not any more difficult or time-consuming, and we both end up happy.

salsa de molcajete

MAKES 3 CUPS (690 G)

Eat this with chips. Or on tacos. Or by the spoonful. It is also great on top of my Black Bean Burgers (page 158) or a "Nacho" Baked Potato (page 156). This recipe makes enough for one bag of tortilla chips—my preferred measurement.

1. Heat a cast-iron pan or griddle over medium-high heat.

2. Toast the tomatoes, turning them every few minutes until all the sides are charred and soft.

3. Add the garlic and chile to the pan and toast until colored and softened.

4. Place the garlic in a mortar and pestle with the salt and mash it into a paste.

5. Add the chiles and fresh cilantro to the mortar and pestle and grind them together with the garlic.

6. Toss in the tomatoes next, bashing them into a chunky paste.

7. Season with lime juice and olive oil. Serve with chips, or as a garnish for tacos (or anything else you choose).

3 medium tomatoes

2 garlic cloves

1 serrano chile

Salt to taste

Fresh cilantro to taste

Juice of 1 lime
(about 1½ to 2 tablespoons)

2 teaspoons olive oil

green tomatillo hot sauce

make two versions of this sauce. Both are almost exactly the same, except one is cooked first, and one is not. This one, the raw one, is the easier of the two. It's spicy hot and pretty amazing (and works well as a salsa, too). Plus leaving it raw makes it the most attractive bright green! If you want to try the cooked version, or the salsa, check out the Variations below.

4 medium tomatillos,
  husks removed*

1 garlic clove

3 to 4 serrano chiles,
  chopped, de-stemsmed**

Handful of cilantro

Squeeze of lime

½ teaspoon salt

Combine everything together in a blender and puree until completely smooth. Serve with any and all of your taco dinners, or you could even use it as a topping for a baked potato (see the "Nacho" Baked Potato on page 156).

Not sure how to buy tomatillos? Look for the smaller ones that are still tightly wrapped in their husks. The big ones are good, too, but the smaller ones taste better.

**Be sure to test the spiciness of your chiles first! With caution, of course. Thankfully, you can usually smell the spice level as soon as you cut one open.*

VARIATIONS:

Try blistering the tomatillos, garlic, chiles, and limes in a hot skillet before blending.

To make this into a chunky salsa instead of a sauce-like salsa verde, chop all the ingredients and combine without pureeing.

TIP FOR LEFTOVERS: Serve this over Easy Tofu Scramble (page 24) or in a breakfast burrito.

asian
curries,
noodles,
& rices

aloo gobi

Aloo gobi, a curry with potatoes and cauliflower, is by far one of my family's favorite Indian dishes. Not only does it require just a handful of ingredients, it's quick to throw together and very easy to transform into a toddler-friendly dish. Serve with rice, naan bread (see page 256 for a homemade recipe), or as is if you're looking for something light.

1½ tablespoons coconut oil

1 small onion, diced

1 tablespoon curry powder

1 teaspoon coriander

½ teaspoon ground cumin or 1 tablespoon whole cumin seed

1 tablespoon fennel seed

2-inch (5 cm) piece of ginger, peeled and grated

4 garlic cloves, grated

1½ cups (350 ml) water

2 medium to large potatoes (any variety is fine, but a creamy potato is preferable), cut into 1-inch (2.5 cm) cubes

1 small head of cauliflower, roughly chopped

½ cup (70 g) fresh or frozen and thawed peas (we use frozen for this)

¼ cup (10 g) chopped cilantro

½ teaspoon salt, or to taste

1. Heat the oil in a large pot over medium heat.

2. Add the onion and cook until translucent and soft, about 8 minutes.

3. Mix in the spices and seeds and stir quickly for about 30 seconds.

4. Add the ginger and garlic and stir for another 30 seconds.

5. Splash in a bit of the water and mix everything together to create a paste.

6. Toss in the potatoes and cauliflower and coat them with the spice paste.

7. Pour in the remaining water and simmer over medium to medium-low heat for 10 to 15 minutes, until the vegetables are tender and most of the liquid is gone.

8. Remove from the heat and mix in the peas and cilantro.

9. Season with salt, then serve.

KID-FRIENDLY TIP: Chop the vegetables into little bite-size pieces and toss them into a bowl with rice before serving. Another great trick is to cook the dish even longer, adding additional liquid as necessary, to make the veggies softer and more palatable.

THE PLANTIFUL TABLE

vegetable curry

SERVES 4 TO 6

Not only is this curry delicious, but it's incredibly good for you! When I was a kid, I would have turned up my nose at all the healthy veggies and spices in this dish, but now it's one of my favorites, especially since it's super-easy, relatively inexpensive, and oh-so-flavorful. Feed it to yourself, your family, or a big tableful of hungry friends!

1. Heat the coconut oil in a large pot over medium heat.

2. Add the onion and cook until translucent.

3. Mix in the pepper and cook for a few more minutes, until they're slightly tender.

4. Add the spices and cook for another minute. If the pot gets too dry, add a splash (about 1 tablespoon) of water.

5. Toss in the garlic and ginger and cook for another 30 seconds.

6. Stir in ½ cup (125 ml) water and mix everything into a paste.

7. Add the salt, tomatoes, zucchini, cauliflower, and carrots, along with the remaining water, and mix.

8. Simmer over medium-low heat until the vegetables are tender, about 15 to 20 minutes.

9. Serve with rice or Naan Bread (see page 256) and enjoy!

KID-FRIENDLY TIP: Have your kid give this a try. The good news is that taste buds change and adjust with age, and anybody can grow to love anything—just as I grew to love this dish.

1½ tablespoons coconut oil

1 small onion, diced

1 cup (175 g) chopped or sliced bell pepper

2 teaspoons curry powder

1 teaspoon cumin seed or ½ teaspoon powdered

2 teaspoons garam masala

½ teaspoon chili powder

1 teaspoon turmeric

1 tablespoon grated garlic

1 tablespoon grated ginger

2½ cups (600 ml) water, divided

1 teaspoon salt, or to taste

1 cup (180 g) chopped tomato (fresh or canned is fine)

1 cup (124 g) cubed or sliced zucchini

1 cup (100 g) chopped cauliflower

1 cup (128 g) cubed or sliced carrots

pho

With its wonderfully flavorful broth, this pho recipe is the perfect vegan alternative to a typically meat-heavy Vietnamese soup. Getting all that flavor packed in, however, requires some time—about an hour and a half to simmer and let the tastes come together. Although this isn't a dish you can make on short notice, it involves very little actual labor, so it's actually pretty high on the "easy" scale. Just get your broth going, then tackle some chores or sit back and relax while it simmers.

PHO

2-inch piece (5 cm) of ginger, peeled

2 large onions, peeled and quartered

1 head of garlic, halved

4 pieces fresh lemongrass

2 carrots, chopped

1 leek, halved lengthwise, rinsed thoroughly, and chopped

1 cup (30 g) dried whole shiitake mushrooms, with stems

4 whole star anise

6 whole cloves

10 whole black peppercorns

2 cinnamon sticks

4 quarts (3.8 L) water, divided

3 tablespoons tamari

8 ounces (227 g) dried bánh phở-style noodles

GARNISHES

Fresh mint

Fresh cilantro

Thai basil

Sliced scallions

Fresh bean sprouts

Thinly sliced red onion

Firm or extra-firm tofu, drained, pressed, and cubed

Lime wedges

Sliced chile pepper (optional)

Chili oil (optional)

1. Set the oven to broil.

2. Place the ginger, onions, garlic, and lemongrass on a roasting sheet, then set the sheet on the top rack in the oven and roast everything for a few minutes, until blistered.

3. Combine all the broth ingredients except the tamari and noodles in a large stockpot and cover with water (about 2 quarts [1.9 L]).

4. Bring to a boil over high heat, then bring the heat down to low and simmer slowly for 1½ hours.

5. Add the tamari and taste for seasoning. Add more if necessary.

6. In a separate pot, bring the remaining water to a boil. Cook the rice noodles according to the package directions.

7. Place a serving size of noodles in a soup bowl and add enough broth to cover them. Add garnishes according to taste.

KID-FRIENDLY TIP: I sometimes skip the herbs and add a small handful of frozen peas and corn to Marlowe's bowl. As an added bonus, the frozen veggies are a great alternative to ice for cooling down a hot bowl of soup.

THE PLANTIFUL TABLE

ramen

This Asian noodle soup boasts a touch of smokiness, making it perfect for fall or winter days. Like the Pho (page 194), this requires a long simmering time but doesn't demand too much real effort on your part once all the veggies are chopped.

RAMEN

2 large onions, peeled and quartered

2 carrots, roughly chopped

1 bunch scallions, roughly chopped or halved

1 cup (30 g) dried whole shiitake mushrooms, with stems

One 4 x 4-inch (10 x 10 cm) sheet dried kombu (dried kelp)*

4 quarts (3.8 L) water, divided

2 tablespoons fresh miso paste

2 teaspoons liquid smoke

2 tablespoons rice wine

¼ cup (60 ml) tamari

12 ounces (340 g, or four 3-ounce [85 g] packages) dried Japanese ramen noodles

GARNISHES

Sliced enoki mushrooms (or your favorite fresh mushrooms)

Sliced fresh scallions

Thinly sliced radish

Fresh miso paste (about 1 teaspoon should do the trick)

1. Combine the onions, carrots, scallions, shiitake, and kombu in a large stockpot and cover completely with water (about 2 quarts [1.9 L]).

2. Bring to a boil over high heat, then lower the heat to medium-low and simmer slowly for 1 hour.

3. Add the miso, liquid smoke, rice wine, and tamari. Taste and adjust seasoning if necessary.

4. In a separate pot, bring the remaining water to a boil. Cook the ramen noodles according to the package directions, drain, and allow them to cool slightly.

5. Assemble the soup with the noodles, broth, and garnishes. Enjoy!

*This edible seaweed can be found in most health food stores or Asian supermarkets.

pad thai

give primary credit for this recipe to Alex, although it's really a mix of what we both love best. The dish contains a healthy amount of vegetables, but I might toss in a few extra—and, as usual, the more fresh herbs the better!

2 tablespoons vegetable oil

1 carrot, julienned

½ cup (55 g) Pickled Daikon (page 249), drained

1 cup (100 g) thinly sliced cauliflower

2 cups (180 g) shredded Napa cabbage

2 teaspoons minced garlic

2 teaspoons minced ginger

4 ounces (114 g) flat rice noodles, soaked in water until soft

2 tablespoons water

1 cup (240 ml) Pad Thai Sauce (recipe follows)

1 tablespoon tamari

½ cup (100 g) pressed, drained, and cubed firm or extra-firm tofu

¼ cup (30 g) sliced scallions

1 tablespoon chopped roasted peanuts

Handful of bean sprouts

Fresh herbs (cilantro, basil, mint) for garnish

A squeeze of fresh lime

1. Preheat a seasoned wok over high heat for several minutes until smoking hot.

2. Add the oil, then add the carrot and pickled daikon and stir-fry for 1 minute.

3. Mix in the cauliflower and cabbage and stir-fry for another minute.

4. Add the garlic and ginger and stir-fry for 1 more minute.

5. Stir in the drained noodles, water, Pad Thai Sauce, and tamari.

6. Boil, stirring continuously, until the liquid has reduced completely and the sauce evenly coats the noodles.

7. Add the tofu, scallions, and chopped peanuts. Toss everything until combined and remove from the heat.

8. Serve immediately, garnished with the bean sprouts, fresh herbs, and lime.

pad thai sauce

MAKES 2 CUPS [480 ML]

½ cup (125 ml) water

½ cup (60 g) dried coconut
palm sugar

1 cup (120 g) tamarind puree

2 tablespoons tamari

1 tablespoon + 1 teaspoon
gochujang
(fermented red chili paste)

½ teaspoon sambal
(chile pepper sauce; optional)

1. Combine the water and palm sugar in a small pot over medium heat and simmer until the sugar has dissolved.

2. Pour the sugar-water into a medium bowl. Add the tamarind, tamari, gochujang, and sambal, if using, and mix to combine.

3. Allow the sauce to cool. Refrigerate until needed.

fried veggie rice

Alex and I like to argue about our rice-to-vegetable ratio in this dish. He's more of a rice man, while I like to add as many veggies as I can. Maybe you agree with Alex and think rice should be the main component, or maybe you're more like me and want the vegetables to be the star. The measurements below meet somewhere in middle, so feel free to adjust to your personal preference.

1. Cook the rice according to package directions. Cool thoroughly by refrigerating overnight.

2. Preheat a seasoned wok over high heat until smoking.

3. Add the oil, then the onion and mushrooms. Stir-fry until the vegetables start to brown.

4. Mix in the carrot, Brussels sprouts, and green beans, and stir-fry for 2 minutes.

5. Add the garlic and ginger, then stir-fry for another minute.

6. Mix in the rice and stir-fry for 1 minute.

7. Add the tamari and stir-fry for 2 minutes, then remove from the heat.

8. Stir in the peas and scallions. Serve.

TIP FOR LEFTOVERS: Eat cold the next day, wearing pajamas.

4 cups (700 g) white long-grain rice (basmati or jasmine)

2 tablespoons vegetable oil

1 small onion, sliced

1 cup (75 g) mushrooms (any variety), sliced

2 tablespoons finely chopped carrot

2 cups (167 g) shredded Brussels sprouts

1 cup (110 g) chopped green beans, blanched

2 teaspoons minced garlic

2 teaspoons minced ginger

¼ cup + 2 tablespoons tamari

½ cup (70 g) peas, blanched

½ cup (60 g) finely sliced scallions

chilled soba

This is my absolutely favorite noodle dish—I could eat it every day. The sauce-covered noodles have just the right amount of acidity, with a nice peanuty, salty-sweet flavor. I've listed my top vegetable choices for the recipe, which I think provide the perfect amount of freshness and crunch to go with the noodles, but you can pick and choose what you (or your kid) want to use. Try it with some thinly sliced spicy peppers mixed in to really kick it up a notch.

4 quarts (3.8 L) water + extra cold water for chilling the noodles

6 ounces (150 g, or 2 bundles) dried soba noodles

1 cup (125 g) shelled edamame

½ cup (70 g) fresh or frozen and thawed peas

½ cup (55 g) fresh green beans, thinly sliced on the bias

1 cup (130 g) julienned cucumber

Handful of freshly chopped herbs (cilantro, Thai basil, mint)

¼ cup (30 g) sliced scallions

Juice of 1 lime (about 1½ to 2 tablespoons)

2 tablespoons chopped peanuts

½ cup (100 g) Miso Peanut Sauce (page 246)

Sliced spicy chiles to taste (one jalapeño usually does the trick; optional)

1. Bring the water to a boil. Cook the soba noodles according to the package directions.

2. When the noodles are done cooking, immediately chill them in cold water, then drain.*

3. Blanch the edamame and peas in boiling water for 30 seconds. Allow them to cool.

4. Combine all the ingredients together in a large bowl and toss until everything is evenly coated with the Miso Peanut Sauce.

5. Serve immediately.

*To get the perfect texture, it's important to cool the noodles right after you cook them.

cashew cheese

MAKES 1 CUP (260 G)

Cheese is a tough topic in the vegan world, so I get asked about it a lot. There are many vegan cheese-replacement options out there, but none are quite the same as good ol' dairy cheese. Sad, I know. The exciting news is that most recipes don't actually need a replacement—they simply don't need cheese. And for those that absolutely do, well, cashew cheese can be a great solution. Although it won't work for all your cheese needs, it does a hell of a magnificent job on pizza. If you've never had it before, I'll understand if you're skeptical, but do give it a try and discover the deliciousness and healthy, unprocessed loveliness that is cashew cheese. Another great thing about this recipe? It's easily freezable, so there's no reason to ever miss out!

Water for soaking the cashews and blending

1 cup (120 g) raw and unsalted cashews

Juice of 1 lemon

1 garlic clove

Small handful of herbs (about 1½ teaspoons of each: oregano, thyme, basil, mint)

1 tablespoon olive oil

½ to 1 teaspoon salt, or to taste

1 tablespoon nutritional yeast (optional)

1. Soak the cashews in a bowl of water for at least 1 hour, preferably overnight. Drain the cashews, reserving the water for later.

2. In a food processor or blender, puree all your ingredients, slowly adding 1 tablespoon of the reserved water at a time to create a creamy consistency. Generally, you will use about 3 tablespoons, but this depends on the amount of time you soaked your cashews—softer nuts will require less water.

3. Continue to blend until the cashews are completely smooth. The smoother, the better—it will create a creamier texture for your pizza. Any chunks, even tiny ones, will dry out more quickly and be harder to digest.

4. Fill a piping bag or plastic bag with the cashew cheese, cut off a bottom corner, and pipe the cheese onto your pizza. You can also just spread the cheese on top using a knife or spatula. Cook the pizza as directed.

THE PLANTIFUL TABLE

pizza:
great alone,
better with
friends.

THE PLANTIFUL TABLE

basic pizza

You want to know how Alex won my heart? Pizza. Well, okay, actually, the first food he ever made for me was tomato soup (see page 124)—and I loved his hair. But after those two things? Pizza. If Alex didn't create his pizzas for me, could I and would I still love him? Er . . . yes. But homemade pizza played a huge role in my falling for him. The first pizza he ever made for me was long before Instagram and probably Twitter, too, but I remember snapping a picture of the most beautiful homemade pizza next to a glass of red wine. Maybe because I was so cool that I was ahead of the Internet food-pic game (just kidding!)? More likely, it's because that day was perfect. That was our second time ever cooking together (read: him cooking for me), and a day I will always remember.

1. Preheat the oven to 550°F (290°C), or the highest setting.

2. Prepare the pizza dough as instructed. Roll it out to a thin layer and place on a dry baking sheet. You can make the pizza whatever size you want (we like to make smaller, individual-size ones).

3. Spread the pizza sauce on the dough, then add the cashew cheese.

4. Drizzle some olive oil over the top, then sprinkle with the salt and garlic.

5. Bake until the crust is golden, about 4 minutes.

6. Remove from the oven, sprinkle with a generous helping of fresh herbs, and enjoy!

Pizza Dough (recipe follows)

Red Pizza Sauce (recipe follows)

Cashew Cheese (page 204) or your preferred cheese

Olive oil to taste

Salt to taste

1 garlic clove, finely minced

Fresh herbs, such as basil, thyme, oregano, to taste

KID-FRIENDLY TIP: Don't tell me your kid doesn't like pizza! Really, though, this should be perfect for little ones.

Recipe continues...

pizza dough

MAKES SIX 12-INCH (30 CM) PIZZAS

PRE-FERMENT

200 g (1½ cups + 1 tablespoon)
all-purpose flour

200 ml (¾ cup + 1½ tablespoons) room-temperature water

Small pinch of instant yeast

DOUGH

Pre-ferment

500 g (4 cups) all-purpose flour

320 ml (1⅓ cups + 1 teaspoon) water

2 g (¾ teaspoon) instant yeast

10 g (½ tablespoon) sea salt

25 ml (1 tablespoon + 2 teaspoons) extra virgin olive oil

The night before making pizza:

1. Combine all the pre-ferment ingredients together in a small bowl. Use a fork or whisk to incorporate until a thick pancake batter like consistency is reached. It does not need to be completely smooth.

2. Cover and let the pre-ferment stand overnight in a cool, dry corner of your kitchen.

At least 3 hours before making pizza:

1. Using a stand mixer with the dough hook attachment, combine the pre-ferment, flour, water, yeast, salt, and oil. Set the mixer to the lowest speed and mix until all ingredients are just combined. Turn the mixer off and allow the dough to rest for 10 minutes.

2. Turn the mixer up to medium speed (I use level four on my KitchenAid) and knead the dough until it's smooth and easily pulls away from the sides of the bowl. Use a spatula to transfer the dough to a lightly oiled plastic container.

3. Fold the dough into thirds by picking up one end and stretching it up and over the middle of the dough. Repeat this with the other side, stretching the seam over to the opposite side. Leave the dough to rise for 1 hour at room temperature.

4. After the dough has rested for 1 hour, fold it into thirds one more time and set aside for another hour.

5. Scrape the dough onto a floured work surface and divide it into six even pieces, each one about 200 g (7 ounces). Sprinkle flour over the dough and shape each piece into a ball (boule). Allow to rest for 20 minutes.

To make the pizza:

1. Move your oven rack to the second slat from the top. Set a pizza stone on the rack. Preheat the oven by setting the broiler to high.

2. Working with one ball of dough at a time, punch it down with your fingertips and begin to stretch it out. You can also use a rolling pin to help get the dough to your desired thickness. Place the dough onto a floured pizza peel, if you have one, or a large cutting board.

3. Now you add whatever sauces or toppings you want—just keep in mind that less can be more.

4. Carefully slide the pizza onto the pizza stone in the oven and bake for 5 to 8 minutes, until the crust just begins to blister.

Note: I've listed metric measurements first for this recipe; as with all yeast dough, I highly recommend using those, if possible, for the best results.

red pizza sauce

MAKES 2 TO 3 CUPS (450 TO 675 G)

28-ounce (794 g) can organic whole peeled tomatoes, liquid drained

1 tablespoon olive oil

1 large garlic clove

Handful of fresh basil

Pinch of fresh oregano

½ teaspoon salt

Freshly cracked black pepper to taste

Puree all the ingredients in a food processor or blender until smooth. Use on your favorite pizza!

pesto potato pizza

I am, by nature, a traditional-pizza kind of girl. The majority of the time I just want red sauce. and cheese (homemade cashew cheese, store-bought vegan cheese, whatever—just give me red sauce and cheese!). I don't really understand it myself, because pesto is one of my favorite things. But I generally skip it on pizza, because red sauce will forever have my heart in that regard. Every once in a while, however, I decide to stray and go to my mistress, pesto. And if I'm being adventurous anyway, why stop at just pesto? I jazz things up a bit and make it an indulgent yet nutritious meal by adding potatoes for hearty creaminess, plus arugula as a healthy green.

Pizza Dough (page 208)

Arugula Basil Pesto (recipe follows)

1 creamer potato, thinly sliced by hand or on a mandoline*

Cashew Cheese (page 204) or other vegan cheese to taste (optional)

Handful of arugula

Fresh lemon juice to taste

Salt to taste

1. Preheat the oven to 550°F (290°C), or the highest setting.

2. Roll out the dough to your desired size and thickness. Move to a baking pan.

3. Spread a layer of pesto across the dough, then add the sliced potato and cheese, if using.

4. Cook until the crust is golden, about 4 minutes.

5. Garnish with arugula and sprinkle with lemon juice and salt before serving.

*Try to find a creamier variety of potato for this pizza (in other words, don't use a baking potato). Slicing it as thin as possible will also help give a smooth texture. If preparing everything in advance, store your sliced potato in cold water until you're ready to use them.

ALLERGY TIP: Nut allergy? No problem. While the toasted pistachios add a wonderful flavor, this pesto does just fine without them.

arugula basil pesto

MAKES 1 TO 2 CUPS (265 TO 530 G)

2 lightly packed cups (30 g)
fresh basil

1 cup (20 g) arugula

½ cup (63 g) pistachios,
shelled and toasted

1 teaspoon salt

¼ cup (60 ml) olive oil

Process all the ingredients together in a food processor or blender for several minutes,
until smooth.

THE PLANTIFUL TABLE

indian mango pizza

borrowed this idea from a friend, but revised the sauce for my family's needs and "veganized" the whole meal. Thanks, Kathleen—my stomach appreciates you, and so does everyone else who tries this recipe.

1. Preheat the oven to 550°F (290°C), or the highest setting.

2. Take out your pre-rolled naan or roll out the pizza dough to your desired thickness. Place it on a baking sheet.

3. Layer on the sauce, then the cashew cheese, then the mango and onion.

4. Cook until the crust is golden, about 4 minutes.

5. Sprinkle with salt and garnish with cilantro before serving.

KID-FRIENDLY TIP: Skip the onion. You can also stir a few tablespoons of yogurt into the sauce to lighten it up even more.

4 to 6 pieces Overnight Naan Bread (page 256) or 1 batch Pizza Dough (page 208)

Indian Spiced Red Sauce (page 243)

Cashew Cheese (page 204), vegan cheese, or other cheese substitute to taste

1 medium mango, sliced

1 small onion, thinly sliced

Salt to taste

Roughly chopped cilantro for garnish

white pizza with caramelized onions & roasted figs

MAKES FOUR 12-INCH (30 CM) PIZZAS

I was a very happy lady when we added this recipe to our pizza rotation. A little bit sweet, a little bit savory—if you ask me, it's the perfect summer pizza. Don't have figs within reach? Grapes can be a great substitute and might make this a bit more approachable for little ones, too!

Pizza Dough (page 208)

Béchamel Sauce
(recipe follows)

Caramelized Onions
(recipe follows)

Handful of figs, halved

Fresh thyme to taste

Salt to taste

1. Preheat the oven to 550°F (290°C), or the highest setting.

2. Roll out the dough to your desired size and thickness. Move to a baking sheet.

3. Spread a generous layer of béchamel sauce across the dough. Add your caramelized onions, then scatter the figs and sprinkle fresh thyme on top.

4. Cook until the dough is golden, about 4 minutes.

5. Sprinkle with salt before serving.

Recipe continues...

THE PLANTIFUL TABLE

savory and sweet!

béchamel sauce

3 tablespoons dairy-free butter
or other butter substitute

3 tablespoons all-purpose flour

2 cups (500 ml) almond milk

1 teaspoon salt

Freshly cracked black pepper
to taste

1. Melt the butter until foamy in a small saucepan over medium heat.

2. Add the flour and whisk into a smooth paste.

3. Simmer the mixture for a few minutes to cook out the taste of flour.

4. Add the milk and bring to a boil, whisking continuously.

5. After the mixture has boiled and thickened, season with salt and pepper. Set aside to cool.

caramelized onions

2 tablespoons olive oil

4 large yellow onions,
very thinly sliced

Salt and black pepper to taste

1. Heat a large heavy-bottomed pot over medium heat.

2. Add the olive oil and the onions. Stir until all the onions are coated with oil.

3. Slowly cook the onions down until they're completely translucent, about 25 minutes.

4. Lower the heat a little and continue cooking for another 30 minutes, stirring every few minutes to prevent the onions from sticking.

5. Eventually the onions will begin to caramelize. Adding a tiny splash of water helps remove any bits that are stuck to the bottom of the pot so they don't burn. The onions will shrink a lot. When they're done, they should be a rich, dark brown and smell of toasted caramel.

6. Season with salt and pepper and set aside to cool until using.

THE PLANTIFUL TABLE

easy pasta with cherry tomatoes & greens

SERVES 4

This is one of the first recipes I put on my blog—complete with the bad night lighting for the photo, no exact ingredient measurements, and a hodgepodge of other issues. It was still a hit, though, which I feel is a pretty good sign that this version will be an even bigger hit! This is another good one for busy moms or anyone, really, who just wants a quick, simple, and delicious meal (which I'm sure you've noticed by now is a trend with me).

1½ tablespoons olive oil + extra for drizzling at the end

1 small to medium onion, thinly sliced

2 pints (300 g) cherry or grape tomatoes, larger tomatoes cut in half

5 garlic cloves, sliced

2 teaspoons balsamic vinegar

1 tablespoon nutritional yeast

½ teaspoon salt

Black pepper to taste

4 to 5 packed cups (120 to 150 g) greens (spinach and arugula)

½ packed cup (10 g) fresh basil + a few additional leaves for garnish

1 tablespoon chopped fresh oregano + a few additional leaves for garnish

A few sprigs of thyme

One 14-ounce (397 g) package of your favorite pasta (or grain), prepared according to package directions

1. Heat the olive oil in a large pan over medium-high heat.

2. Add the onion and cook for a few minutes, until translucent.

3. Mix in the cherry tomatoes and allow them to blister.

4. After a few minutes, add the garlic and stir.

5. Mix in the balsamic vinegar.

6. Add the nutritional yeast, salt, and pepper and stir.

7. Toss in the spinach, arugula, and herbs and cook until the greens have wilted.

8. Combine the sauce with the cooked pasta, then add a drizzle of olive oil, garnish with extra fresh herbs, and serve.

lemony vegetable & herb pasta

This is what I make when I'm wondering, "What can I do with all these wonderful, half-used-up vegetables?" It's similar to the 15-Minute Vegetable Couscous (page 146), in that you can pretty easily change up many of the vegetables in the dish to fit the foods you have left in your fridge. It's different, however, in that it takes a bit more time and is best eaten with the ones you love—not scarfed down by yourself while sitting on the couch (though it's just as good that way, too). Hate eggplant? No problem: skip it. Need to use up some extra kale? That would be perfect—just make sure to chop it small. Don't skip the garlic, tomatoes, or any other of the seasoning factors, and you'll be set. I recommend enjoying it with a glass of chilled white wine, since you're using wine in the recipe, anyway . . . a little for the sauce, a little for you!

One 14- to 16-ounce (397 to 454 g) package of your favorite pasta

2 tablespoons olive oil + extra for drizzling at the end

1 small onion, small diced

1 small carrot, finely diced

1 cup (75 g) sliced mushrooms (use your favorite kind, or whatever you have on hand)

4 garlic cloves, sliced

1 cup (124 g) diced zucchini

1 cup (82 g) cubed eggplant

1 cup (83 g) shredded Brussels sprouts

1½ teaspoons salt

Black pepper to taste

1 cup (150 g) quartered cherry tomatoes

1 cup (250 ml) white wine

1 cup (250 ml) Vegetable Stock (page 116)

Juice and zest of 1 lemon

Two small handfuls of fresh herbs, or to taste

1. Prepare the pasta according to the package directions, making sure to keep it al dente so that it still has a bit of bite to it—you don't want it too soft.

2. Heat the olive oil in a large sauté pan over medium-high heat.

3. Sauté the onion, carrot, and mushrooms until the vegetables are lightly colored.

4. Add the garlic and cook for another minute.

5. Mix in the zucchini, eggplant, and shredded Brussels sprouts and sauté for a few more minutes, until the vegetables begin to soften.

6. Season with the salt and a few cracks of pepper, then mix in the cherry tomatoes.

7. Add the white wine to deglaze the pan.

8. Allow the wine to boil and reduce until almost completely evaporated.

9. Mix in the cooked pasta.

10. Add the vegetable stock and cook until the liquid has reduced and you're left with a light sauce.

11. Remove from the heat, then add the lemon juice and zest and the herbs.

12. Drizzle with olive oil before serving.

hearty green pesto pasta

SERVES 4

Pesto (and green food in general) is a favorite in our home, which is why I've included multiple versions in this cookbook—you should check out the Pea Pesto (page 52) and the Arugula-Basil Pesto (page 211), too. I'm not sure why, when, or how kids are programmed to believe that green foods are gross foods, but I know it happens with a lot of children. Hoping to avoid this with our daughter, we started promoting green foods as fun foods in this house from the get-go, and it appears to have worked pretty well. If we leave it up to Marlowe, she'll choose green soup or green pasta 98 percent of the time. I'm devoted to red sauces myself (see page 243 for my go-to recipe), but I'll never pass on pesto pasta.

¼ cup (30 g) raw cashews

½ cup (125 ml) olive oil

1 bunch kale, stemmed*

1 packed cup (20 g) fresh basil

Juice of ½ lemon (about 1 tablespoon)

2 tablespoons nutritional yeast

Up to 1 cup (250 ml) almond milk

1 teaspoon salt

Black pepper to taste

One 14- to 16-ounce (397 to 454 g) package of your favorite pasta, prepared according to package directions

1. Combine the cashews and the oil in a food processor and blend until creamy.

2. Add the kale, basil, lemon juice, and nutritional yeast to the food processor with the cashews and blend until smooth.

3. Pour the mixture into a medium pot and place over medium-low heat. Slowly stir in the almond milk, adding just enough to turn it into a sauce, and simmer over low heat for 5 to 10 minutes. Season with salt and pepper.

4. Toss with the prepared pasta until evenly coated. Serve and enjoy!

*This recipe calls for kale, but we often use whatever extra (non-watery) greens we have in our garden. Beet greens are another favorite and add a touch of welcome bitterness to the recipe.

KID-FRIENDLY TIP: One of my greatest pleasures is watching Marlowe cut her own greens from the garden, help wash them, and practically make the pesto all on her own—and then devour it, of course. If possible, having your child pick the leaves themselves creates so much more excitement, even if it's from a simple potted basil plant on your windowsill.

TIP FOR LEFTOVERS: If you have extra pesto, it's excellent spread on toast, added to sandwiches, or used in place of the pistachio pesto in the Pesto Potato Pizza (page 210). It's also super-easy to freeze for a later date. Simply pull your container of pesto out of the freezer when you'd like to use it and allow it to defrost a bit on the counter before reheating in a small pot.

THE PLANTIFUL TABLE

kale & sun-dried tomato pasta

SERVES 4

Do you like sun-dried tomatoes? Me, too! In fact, I love-love-love them. This dish is really quick to make and incredibly enjoyable to eat.

1. Process 2 tablespoons of the olive oil* with the walnuts, sun-dried tomatoes, and garlic in a food processor until mostly smooth but not too creamy.

2. Heat the remaining tablespoon of oil in a large pot over medium heat. Add the onion and cook until translucent.

3. Stir in the kale and a splash of water and cook for 1 to 2 minutes, until the kale has wilted. Check the seasoning and adjust if necessary.

4. Remove from the heat; add the sun-dried tomato mixture and the pasta water. Stir until well blended.

5. Add the pasta, mix well, and serve.

Feel free to use the oil from the tomato jar for cooking and mixing. The oil can also be used throughout the week in other dishes, so don't just drain and toss it!

TIP FOR LEFTOVERS: Chances are you won't have any sauce left over, but if you do, it makes a wonderful sandwich spread.

3 tablespoons olive oil, divided*

½ cup (50 g) walnuts

1½ cups (about one 10-ounce [284 g] jar) sun-dried tomatoes packed in oil*

2 garlic cloves

1 small onion, small diced

1 bunch kale, stemmed and chopped

Salt to taste

½ cup (160 ml) water reserved from cooking pasta

One 14- to 16-ounce (397 to 454 g) package of your favorite pasta, prepared according to package directions, with water drained and saved

olive pasta even a toddler will love

SERVES 4

It took me a long time to fall in love with olives. Some people adore them, some people hate them, and some, like me, will eventually come around. I am now a full-on olive lover. Marlowe, like many kids, still very much dislikes them . . . but she sure does love this recipe. It's hard not to—it's rich, creamy, salty, and delicious. I recommend trying it for yourself, even if you don't think you're a fan of olives. You may be surprised.

One and a half 15-ounce (170 g) cans of olives (your favorite variety), pitted and drained + extra for garnish*

2 garlic cloves

A few leaves of fresh thyme + extra for garnish

Juice of ½ lemon (about 1 tablespoon)

1 teaspoon Dijon or yellow mustard

3 tablespoons olive oil

1 tablespoon dairy-free butter (optional)

1 small onion, small diced

1 tablespoon all-purpose flour

1 tablespoon nutritional yeast + extra for garnish

¼ cup (60 ml) water

¼ cup (60 ml) dairy-free milk

1 teaspoon salt, or to taste

One 14-ounce (397 g) package of pasta (your favorite variety), cooked as directed on packaging

Fresh parsley to taste

1. Combine the olives, garlic, thyme, lemon juice, mustard, and olive oil in a food processor (saving some extra olives and thyme for garnish) and blend until just combined—you want the mixture to be a bit chunky.

2. Melt the butter in a medium pot over medium-low heat. Add the onion and cook until translucent and soft, about 5 minutes.

3. Mix in the flour and nutritional yeast to create a roux. Quickly add the water and milk, stirring constantly until the flour is completely incorporated and a white sauce forms.

4. Add the olive mixture and simmer for a few minutes, until it slightly thickens. Season with salt.

5. Add the pasta and simmer for another minute.

6. Garnish with thyme, parsley, and/or chopped olives and a sprinkle of nutritional yeast before serving.

TIP: You can use the full two cans of olives, if you want. If you love olives, I highly recommended it!

THE PLANTIFUL TABLE

mushroom bolognese

This rich, flavorful, slow-cooked sauce is special enough to impress friends or a date. As an added bonus, even picky eaters will enjoy it—although the recipe name features the word "mushroom," the taste is very well-rounded, rather than a mushroom explosion in your mouth. Like many traditional Italian sauces, this needs to cook for a while to allow the flavors to fully develop. To pass the time while this simmers on the stove and spreads its heady aroma, I suggest you set the table, light a candle, and sip some wine.

1. Heat the oil in a large pot over medium heat. Add the mushrooms and cook for 20 minutes, until the liquid has evaporated.

2. Mix in a few sprigs of the thyme and cook for another minute.

3. Stir in the onion, celery, and carrots and cook for 20 minutes, until the vegetables are nice and soft.

4. Add the tomato paste, blend well, and cook for another 1 to 2 minutes.

5. Pour in the wine and scrape the bottom of the pan to deglaze it. Cook for another minute.

6. Add the water and simmer, covered, over low heat for 30 minutes.

7. Mix in the sherry vinegar, then season with parsley and basil.

8. Toss the sauce with the cooked pasta and serve.

1 tablespoon olive oil

Two 14-ounce (400 g) packages of mushrooms (any kind), pureed or finely minced

A few sprigs of fresh thyme

1 onion, small diced

1 celery stalk, small diced

2 carrots, small diced

3 tablespoons tomato paste

½ cup (125 ml) red wine

1 cup (250 ml) water

½ teaspoon sherry vinegar

Fresh parsley to taste

Fresh basil to taste

One 14- to 16-ounce (397 to 454 g) package of your favorite pasta (I recommend penne for this), prepared according to package directions

artichoke, garlic, & cashew ravioli

MAKES 25 TO 30 RAVIOLI

Who doesn't love ravioli, those little pillow-y pockets stuffed with goodness? I'm definitely in! I admit right off the bat that, unlike most of my other pasta dishes, this isn't the quickest recipe. It's not a meal to make after a long day of work, classes, or other tiring things—it's intended for a day where you want to do nothing but enjoy (somewhat messy) cooking (and eating). We don't make this nearly often enough in our house due to time constraints, but it is certainly loved by all: parents, toddlers, grandparents, and anyone else lucky enough to be part of our occasional ravioli adventure. This recipe works well with a pasta maker, but it's entirely possible to do it by hand, too.

PASTA DOUGH

2 cups (250 g) all-purpose flour

1 teaspoon salt

1¼ tablespoons olive oil

1 cup (250 ml) water

FILLING

¼ cup (30 g) raw cashews

1 garlic clove

1 tablespoon olive oil

One 14-ounce (400 g) can artichoke hearts, rinsed and drained

1 scallion

2 tablespoons nutritional yeast

1 tablespoon lemon juice

½ to 1 teaspoon salt, or to taste

FOR SERVING

2 cups (500 g) Our Go-to Red Sauce (page 242), or your favorite pasta sauce

Drizzle of olive oil

Fresh herbs (such as basil, oregano, or even a few small pieces of mint) for garnish

To Make the Pasta Dough

1. Combine the flour and salt in a large bowl.

2. Add the olive oil and water, mixing until a
   ball of dough forms.

3. Knead the dough on a floured surface until
   smooth, 3 to 5 minutes.

4. Cover the dough in plastic wrap and store
   in the fridge until needed, or make the
   ravioli right away.

To Make the Filling

1. Combine the cashews, garlic, and oil in a
   food processor. Blend into a puree, scraping
   down the sides occasionally, until the
   cashews are as smooth as possible.

2. Add three-quarters of the artichokes and
   all the other filling ingredients and puree
   completely.

3. If you like a more textured filling, roughly
   chop the remaining artichokes and mix
   them into the pureed mixture by hand. If
   you're aiming for a smoother filling (which
   might be a bit more kid-friendly), add all
   the remaining artichokes into the food
   processor and blend until smooth.

To Make the Ravioli

1. Once the dough and filling are both ready,
   prepare the work surface. You want a flat,
   dry, well-floured area to make the ravioli.

Recipe continues...

2. Begin by sectioning off the dough into four pieces, using a dough cutter or sharp knife. Then, one section at a time, begin rolling out your dough into 1/8-inch (3 mm) thick flat sheets. Dust with flour as needed. I recommend using a pasta machine at this point, if you have one. If you don't, no worries: you can still make ravioli magic—just roll the dough out as thin as possible!

3. Drop 1 tablespoon of filling every 2 inches (5 cm) apart on one half of a rolled out sheet of dough.

4. Lightly fold the other half of the dough on top of the side with the filling. Using your fingers, gently press around each mound of filling to form your ravioli. Try to remove as much air as possible without breaking the dough or squeezing the filling out of its pocket.

5. Use a sharp knife or dough cutter to slice each pillow into a square (or triangle or circle!). Gently press the edges closed with a fork to form a tight seal.

6. Repeat steps 3 to 5 until you run out of dough and/or filling.

7. Fill a large pot with water and salt it generously. Bring to a boil.

8. Cook the ravioli in small batches in the boiling water. Do not overcrowd the pot, or the ravioli will stick together and tear. The pasta will float when it's done cooking—it typically takes between 2 to 4 minutes, depending on the size of the ravioli.

9. Gently remove the ravioli from water using a strainer or large slotted spoon. Serve with your preferred sauce and garnish with olive oil and fresh herbs.

KID-FRIENDLY TIP: (Most) kids love to get their hands dirty—this is a great recipe for that. If you're anything like me, there will be flour everywhere, whether a toddler is present or not, so enjoy the messiness and consider it time well spent. Make those memories, and watch your kids want to eat something they so actively helped create.

it's a
ravioli
adventure!

THE PLANTIFUL TABLE

butternut squash lasagna

This dish is a truly brilliant vegan entree. Combined with the white cream and red sauce, the butternut squash practically melts right into the lasagna, making it an ideal "hidden veggie" dish for kids. And since the squash bakes through directly in the pan, you're saved the extra step of cooking it first. I grew up with a plain sauce-and-cheese lasagna, but my mom definitely could have gotten away with feeding this to me.

1. Make the white cream first by blending all the ingredients together with a food processor or blender until very creamy, adding a touch more milk if necessary to reach the correct smooth consistency.

2. Preheat the oven to 350°F (175°C).

3. Peel and de-seed the butternut squash, then slice it very, very thin. Brush olive oil all over the squash. Sprinkle it with the salt and thyme.

4. In an oven-safe baking dish, layer the Red Sauce, squash, White Cream, and pasta noodles until all the sauce is used up.

5. When you're done layering the ingredients, sprinkle the bread crumbs on top, then add a heavy drizzle of olive oil and a sprinkling of salt and thyme.

6. Cover with aluminum foil and cook for 35 minutes, then remove the foil and cook for another 10 minutes, until the squash is cooked through.

WHITE CREAM

One 14-ounce (400 g) can butter beans (lima beans), drained

2 to 3 tablespoons olive oil

¾ teaspoon salt

¼ cup (60 ml) almond milk

2 to 3 teaspoons nutritional yeast

1 tablespoon chopped fresh thyme

LASAGNA

1 small butternut squash

Olive oil to taste

Salt to taste

Fresh thyme to taste

Our Go-to Red Sauce (page 242), simmered for 5 minutes instead of 15 minutes

White Cream

One 9-ounce (255 g) box no-boil lasagna

⅓ cup (37 g) dried or (33 g) fresh bread crumbs

mac & cheese

I could make this recipe one-handed, with my eyes closed. Marlowe probably could, too, with a little help with the chopping and cooking. I've improved upon this recipe throughout the years, and I'm pretty sure it's perfect at this point. When I cook for friends, 92 percent of the time they request this meal. This is great for me, because I could eat it every day. The most amazing thing about this recipe is not only that it's not bad for you, like a lot of mac and cheeses, but that it's actually pretty good for you! It's cholesterol-free (like every recipe in this plant-based cookbook), and it's also packed with protein and nutrient-filled vegetables. Don't let this health factor scare you away, though—I promise you, it's rich, creamy, and intensely comforting, making it a pleasure to sit down with a bowl.

One 14- to 16-ounce (397 to 454 g) package of your favorite pasta (we like to use shells for this)

2 carrots, chopped (about ¾ to 1 cup [96 to 128 g])

1 small onion, roughly chopped (about ¾ cup [120 g])

1 cup (205 g) roughly chopped butternut squash

1 medium to large potato (creamer or red; not a baking potato), roughly chopped (about 1½ cups [225 g])

3 to 3½ cups (700 to 825 ml) water

6 tablespoons dairy-free butter, divided

½ cup (60 g) raw cashews

1 garlic clove

Pinch of cayenne pepper (optional)

1 cup (160 g) nutritional yeast + extra for topping

1 tablespoon lemon juice

Salt and black pepper to taste

½ cup (50 g) fresh bread crumbs

Spicy smoked Spanish paprika to taste

1. Preheat the oven to 375°F (190°C).

2. Prepare the pasta according to the package directions and set aside.

Recipe continues...

3. Place the carrots, onion, butternut squash, and potato in a large pot and fill it with enough water to cover all the vegetables. Bring to a boil.

4. Once boiling, reduce the heat down to a simmer and cook until all the vegetables are soft, about 10 to 15 minutes, depending on the size of the vegetables. Do not drain the water when they're done.

5. In a blender, puree 5 tablespoons of the butter with the cashews, garlic, and cayenne, if using. If more liquid is required, slowly add a little water from the simmered vegetables to the mixture and puree until creamy. It's important to make sure the cashews are completely smooth.

6. Add the cooked vegetables and the nutritional yeast and blend until fully incorporated.

7. Slowly add the leftover water from the simmered vegetables and blend until you create a velvety, "cheesy" sauce.

8. Mix in the lemon juice, then season with the salt and pepper.

9. Combine the sauce with the prepared pasta—add as much as you want. In my opinion? More sauce is better!

10. Place the mac and cheese in an oven-safe dish.

11. Melt the remaining tablespoon of butter in a small pan over medium heat, then add the bread crumbs and lightly toast them for 1 to 2 minutes, tossing frequently, until golden.

12. Sprinkle the toasted bread crumbs over the pasta, then top with the paprika and a sprinkle of nutritional yeast.

13. Cover with aluminum foil and bake for 10 minutes. Remove the foil and broil for about a minute, until the top is golden brown.

14. Serve hot, and enjoy this creamy goodness!

HEALTHY TIP: Although this is already pretty good for you as far as mac and cheese goes, if you want to make an even healthier version, you can substitute cauliflower for the potato.

TIP FOR LEFTOVERS: When possible, I like to put double or single portions of this mac and cheese in containers to freeze. That way, on the cold, rainy days when I don't want to think about feeding everyone, I can just set it on the counter to defrost for a few hours beforehand and then reheat. You can easily heat this back up on the stove—I like to warm a bit of almond milk, maybe ¼ cup (60 ml) or so, in a pot first and then add the defrosted pasta and a sprinkle of nutritional yeast to it, mixing everything as it heats. It becomes extra-creamy and delicious. Just be careful not to overcook the pasta, so it doesn't turn to mush!

BONUS TIP FOR LEFTOVERS: Have leftover sauce? Great! Use it in quesadillas, nachos, or whatever else you might want to add a "cheesy" sauce to!

dressings,
sauces, &
toppings

balsamic vinaigrette

'll admit it: sometimes I don't serve salad simply because I don't feel like going the extra step to make a dressing—which is all kinds of crazy, since it takes only about three minutes to make dressing magic happen. For whatever reason, I don't mind spending an hour on soup, but I loathe taking those extra three minutes on a salad, even though it's delicious and healthy. My next New Year's resolution is to stop worrying about the amount of effort and just make more salads. With this dressing, that should be easy.

¼ cup (60 ml) balsamic vinegar

Juice of ½ lemon (about 1 tablespoon)

1 tablespoon + 1 teaspoon Dijon mustard

1 garlic clove, finely chopped or minced

2 tablespoons + 1 teaspoon honey or agave syrup

½ cup (125 ml) olive oil

Place all the ingredients in a jar with tight-fitting lid and shake until well combined, or you can blend everything together in a food processor. I recommend serving this with Roasted Vegetable Salad (page 106), or try it with anything else you like—balsamic vinaigrette is incredibly versatile!

A NOTE ABOUT THIS RECIPE

I'm sure there are a few good store-bought balsamic vinaigrette options out there, but I always make my own so I can control exactly what goes into it. My best tip, though, for buying commercial salad dressings is to read the labels. You'll be surprised to see that, more often than not, they're made primarily of sugar. Although this homemade version isn't sugar-free (we use honey or agave syrup), it's a much, much healthier, unprocessed alternative to the store-bought stuff. So make yourself a batch of this and store it in your fridge to use throughout the week. You'll never need store-bought balsamic vinaigrette again.

sherry vinaigrette

MAKES 1 CUP (235 G)

We never used a lot of sherry vinegar in our house until a few years ago, when, right before Christmas, Alex mentioned that he wanted to get some the next time we went to the store. So I grabbed a fancy bottle from the market, wrapped it up, and put it in his stocking. We started using it all the time, and it's been a household favorite ever since. We both love it; I just don't think we ever bothered to buy it for our pantry before. But I'm happy we've found a new pantry staple . . . and this dressing? It's my favorite. If you don't use a food processor, it's easy enough for a toddler to make.

Place all the ingredients into a jar with a tight-fitting lid. Shake-shake-shake until well combined, or you can blend everything together in a food processor. Serve with the Bread Salad (page 102), Roasted Vegetable Salad (page 106), or your favorite everyday salad!

¼ cup (60 ml) sherry vinegar

Juice of ½ lemon
  (about 1 tablespoon)

1 tablespoon + 1 teaspoon
  Dijon mustard

1 garlic clove, very finely
  chopped or minced

Chopped fresh thyme to taste

2 tablespoons + 1 teaspoon
  honey or agave syrup

½ cup (125 ml) olive oil

our go-to red sauce

MAKES 2 CUPS (500 G)

When we want a good, classic, not-overly-fussy red sauce for our pasta, this is our go-to recipe. It's quick, easy, flavorful, and impossible to mess up. My top advice: season well, and don't skimp on the olive oil.

2 tablespoons olive oil

1 small onion, small diced

3 garlic cloves, sliced

Large handful of fresh basil, chopped

Small handful of fresh oregano, chopped

A few sprigs of fresh thyme

One 28-ounce (794 g) can crushed tomatoes

¾ teaspoon salt, or to taste

1. Heat the oil in a medium pot over medium heat, making sure the bottom of the pot is completely coated with oil.

2. Add the onion and sauté until translucent, about 5 minutes.

3. Mix in the garlic and cook for a minute or so, making sure not to burn the garlic.

4. Add the herbs and cook for another 30 seconds.

5. Mix in the tomatoes and simmer for 15 to 20 minutes, until it reaches your desired consistency.

6. Season with salt and pour over your favorite type of pasta—or use it however you want.

KID-FRIENDLY TIP: It's pretty easy to sneak a few vegetables into this sauce—just small-dice or shred some carrots or zucchini and add them at the same time as the tomatoes.

TIP FOR LEFTOVERS: This is perfect for pizzas, sauces, and soup bases—such as the Bread Soup (page 124) or the Smoky White Bean & Black Rice Soup with Kale Chips (page 132). We also use it in our Stewed Chickpeas & Okra (page 148).

indian spiced red sauce

This is the sauce base for our Indian Mango Pizza (page 213), and it's also great stewed with okra, chickpeas, or just about any vegetable, and served with naan bread (see page 256 for a homemade recipe) or another flat bread.

Puree all the ingredients together in a blender until smooth.

1½ cups (380 g) Our Go-to Red Sauce (page 242) or pureed canned, crushed tomatoes

½ teaspoon coriander

½ teaspoon cumin seed

½ teaspoon chili powder

1 teaspoon olive oil

1 tablespoon rice vinegar or apple cider vinegar

1 garlic clove

1 teaspoon salt, if using canned tomatoes

marlowe's favorite ginger sauce

MAKES ½ CUP (60 G)

Alternate title: Everyone's Favorite Sauce. One day I offered Marlowe a piece of cauliflower as I was making this sauce. She must have dipped it into the mixing bowl, and that concoction stuck—"cauliflower and sauce," one of her favorites. Personally, I'd rather eat it with an egg roll, but, hey, if she wants a plain, raw veggie, I'm not complaining! Almost every friend and family member has said the same thing about the sauce: "I could just drink this." Although I wouldn't recommend that method, it is that good!

1 tablespoon + 1 teaspoon soy sauce or Bragg's Liquid Aminos

1 tablespoon + 1 teaspoon apple cider vinegar

1 teaspoon sesame oil

2 teaspoons honey or agave syrup

1 tablespoon lime juice

1 garlic clove, grated

1-inch (2.5 cm) piece of ginger, grated

2 to 3 tablespoons water

Combine all the ingredients in a bowl until well mixed, adding enough water to reach your desired consistency. Serve as a dipping sauce for raw cauliflower, as a salad dressing, or however your heart desires!

TIP FOR LEFTOVERS: Sometimes I'll use this as a sauce base for an Asian-inspired noodle dish.

more,
please!

miso peanut sauce

MAKES 1¼ CUPS (250 G)

This is another one of Marlowe's most-loved sauces, second only to her favorite ginger sauce (page 244). A very easy recipe to make, it can really do no wrong. It tastes absolutely fantastic served over noodles (such as in our Chilled Soba dish on page 202) or as a salad dressing. I also sometimes serve this as a dipping sauce for baked tofu for Marlowe.

5 tablespoons creamy peanut butter

1 tablespoon + 1 teaspoon fresh miso paste

1 tablespoon + 1 teaspoon sesame oil

¼ cup (60 ml) rice wine vinegar

½ cup (125 ml) water

2 tablespoons fresh lime juice

1 tablespoon + 1 teaspoon tamari

Mix everything together in a medium bowl until the miso and peanut butter are fully combined and the sauce is smooth.

mango cilantro sauce

MAKES ¾ CUP (90 G)

More simple than the Mango Chutney (page 248), this makes a great, super-fast option to serve as a refreshing sauce or topping for spicy meals. Serve with Lentil Fritters (page 82) or as a topping for Black Bean Burgers (page 158).

½ ripe mango

¼ cup (10 g) chopped cilantro*

½ teaspoon salt

1½ tablespoons apple cider vinegar

Juice from ½ lime (about 1 tablespoon)

2 garlic cloves

1 to 2 tablespoons water

Combine all the ingredients in a food processor and blend until smooth.

Hate cilantro? Use mint instead.

mango chutney

MAKES 1½ CUPS (340 G)

Come mango season in Florida, this chutney is a lifesaver. If you live in a region where 50+ mangoes somehow wind up in your house on any given day, then this recipe is made especially for you. Not in a place where the mangoes are coming out your ears in the summer? This recipe is still worth a trip to the store for a mango (or five). We love using it as a dipping sauce for Lentil Fritters (page 82) or serving it with any spicy dish as a sweet, refreshing topping. Depending on the ripeness of your mango, you probably won't need the optional sweetener that I've listed, since mangoes are naturally packed with sugar. I prefer to avoid adding sugar to my food whenever possible, but sometimes just a bit helps a lot!

½ small onion, diced

1 medium to large mango, diced

1½ teaspoons grated or minced ginger

½ teaspoon garam masala

1 tablespoon sugar (optional; usually not recommended)

1½ tablespoons lemon juice

2½ tablespoons white wine vinegar or apple cider vinegar

1 tablespoon water

Pinch of salt

Combine all the ingredients in a small pot and simmer over medium-low heat for about 20 minutes, until the onion is soft. Allow the chutney to cool, then refrigerate. Serve chilled.

TIP: Have lots of mangoes? Make tons of chutney and try your hand at canning it. Everyone loves a sweet, homemade "just because" gift!

pickled daikon

only grew to love all things pickled a few years ago; these days, I can't get enough. My mouth waters just thinking about pickled radishes. Mmmm. This is a very easy recipe for a quick pickle; it's not something you jar and eat months from now (not that it would last that long in this house anyway). I've included pickled daikon in a few of the Asian dishes in this book, such as Pad Thai (page 198) or Bánh Mì Chay (page 74), but you could try leaving out the sambal and ginger and adding this to tacos, as well. It's a wonderful garnish for almost anything, and it also works well on its own as a snack.

Combine all the ingredients except the daikon in a medium bowl and stir until the sugar is completely dissolved. Add the daikon and combine thoroughly. Allow the mixture to pickle overnight in the refrigerator before serving. Keep refrigerated.

½ cup (125 ml) rice vinegar

¼ cup (60 ml) water

2 tablespoons sugar

½ teaspoon sambal (chile pepper sauce)

1 tablespoon minced ginger

¼ teaspoon mustard seed

1 medium daikon radish, julienned

napa cabbage & daikon kimchi

MAKES 1 PACKED QUART [4 CUPS [800 G]]

Oh, kimchi, what a spicy, delicious thing you are. Kimchi is one of those Asian foods that's hard to find without fish sauce in it. Luckily, in no way, shape, or form does it need fish sauce, so I put together this simple and yummy (and sometimes messy to make) recipe for all the Nemo lovers out there.

1 medium head of Napa cabbage

2 tablespoons salt

¼ cup (57 g) sugar

20 garlic cloves, minced

2- to 3-inch (5 to 8 cm) piece of ginger, peeled and minced

¼ cup (60 ml) tamari

¼ cup (60 ml) water

½ cup Korean chili powder

2 tablespoons gochujang (fermented red chili paste)

½ medium daikon radish, julienned

1. Slice the cabbage in half lengthwise; then slice it in half again to make quarters. Remove the core of the cabbage from the base, then slice the cabbage width-wise into ½-inch (1.25 cm) pieces. Place the cabbage in a large bowl and toss with the salt and sugar. Marinate for at least 1 hour.

2. Chop the garlic and ginger in a food processor, then place it in a large bowl and stir in the tamari, water, Korean chili powder, and gochujang. Set aside.

3. Drain all the excess water from the cabbage and combine it with the daikon and chili paste mixture. Marinate overnight before serving. Store in the refrigerator for up to 2 weeks.

KID-FRIENDLY TIP: Please send me any and all pictures of kids eating kimchi. I want to see them! (Instagram: @ohdeardrea)

ketchup

MAKES 4 CUPS (960 G)

A timeless American staple, and much loved in my house. This recipe has a long ingredient list, but I assure you, it's easy to make—and it creates a lot, so you can easily keep some on hand. If ketchup is one of those things you can't avoid having at pretty much every meal, at least you can feel better by making it yourself, right?

2 tablespoons olive oil

1 teaspoon fennel seed

1 tablespoon coriander seed

½ teaspoon mustard seed

1 teaspoon cumin seed

1 large red onion, diced

2 small carrots, diced

8 garlic cloves, smashed

10 plum tomatoes, roughly chopped

2 tablespoons tomato paste

¾ cup (150 g) brown sugar

½ cup (125 ml) apple cider vinegar

¼ cup (60 ml) soy sauce

2 tablespoons salt

Freshly cracked black pepper to taste

2 cups (500 ml) water

1. Heat the olive oil in a large pot over medium-low heat.

2. Add the seeds, onion, carrots, and garlic and cook for 15 minutes, until the vegetables are sweating and very fragrant.

3. Mix in the remaining ingredients and bring to a boil. Lower the heat and simmer for 20 minutes.

4. Puree the mixture, then strain to make sure it's extra-creamy.

5. Simmer the sauce again over low heat until thick and shiny, then strain once more.

6. Bottle, can, or freeze!

A NOTE ABOUT THIS RECIPE

Dear Ketchup,
*   We love you. You're the best.*
Yours truly,
(almost) Everyone

That's all I was going to say about ketchup, because I thought it got the point across. But then Alex came into the room to proofread, and he was, like, "That's it?! That's all you're writing about ketchup?" So let me add more for good measure: ketchup is so good and so bad for so many reasons. I'd be lying if I didn't tell you that sometimes we offer Marlowe ketchup just so she'll finish a meal. It's very rare, but it does happen. You've probably noticed that a lot of the recipes in this book feature ketchup in the photos or as a recommended accompaniment, such as the Shepherd's Pie (page 138) or Calentado (page 48)—these are all dishes that I like serving with ketchup. Not because I'm afraid Marlowe wouldn't finish the meal otherwise, but because I grew up expecting ketchup with them, and, even now, as an adult in my thirties, I enjoy them with ketchup. I grew up that way and stayed that way—that's kind of how it works, which is even more reason to get your kids conditioned to eat and enjoy good food now. Is it impossible to change food habits? Absolutely not, but it's easier the younger you start.

citrus ponzu

MAKES ⅓ CUP (80 ML)

Kids love dipping sauces just as much as adults do . . . food instantly becomes more fun when you have something to dunk it into! This recipe is a nice, light option and goes wonderfully with just about anything you can think to dip. We like to serve it with the Mushroom Pot Stickers (page 89), or basically any fresh vegetables we have on hand.

1 tablespoon tamari

2 teaspoons fresh lime juice

1 teaspoon fresh lemon juice

1 tablespoon fresh orange juice

1 teaspoon raw honey or agave syrup

2 teaspoons rice vinegar or apple cider vinegar

1 tablespoon water

½ teaspoon sesame oil

¼ teaspoon chili oil (optional)

Combine all of the ingredients together in a medium bowl and mix until fully incorporated.

breads,
etc.

overnight naan bread

Does the term "pre-ferment"* make you as nervous as it makes me? Bread in general, no matter what kind, can be a bit intimidating to make from scratch—I think I cried the first time I ever attempted it. As you slowly learn the process, you'll realize that it doesn't need to make you anxious and that it's actually very doable. Just read through the instructions, be sure you measure everything exactly (I recommend using the metric measurements for best results, so I listed them first when applicable), and have fun. Your world doesn't depend on it—a big bolt of lightning won't strike you if you mess something up—it's just bread. Starting off with something easy, such as this naan recipe, is a good idea. When made properly, it will be light, airy, and oh-so-tender. Even if it's not perfect and looks a bit deflated or on the dense side, people are unlikely to notice; since it's already a flat bread, you'll be in the clear. Serve this with your favorite Indian meals, such as the Vegetable Curry (page 193), or make a sandwich out of it. You can also use it as the base for the Indian Mango Pizza (page 213).

PRE-FERMENT

200 g (1½ cups + 1 tablespoon) bread flour

200 ml (¾ cup + 1½ tablespoons) room temperature water

⅛ teaspoon instant yeast

DOUGH

Pre-ferment

300 ml (1¼ cups) room temperature water

500 g (4 cups) bread flour

2 g (¾ teaspoon) instant yeast

2 tablespoons olive oil

12 g (2 teaspoons) sea salt

1. The night before you plan on baking the naan, mix all the pre-ferment ingredients together in a large bowl until they reach a thick batter consistency. Cover the bowl and let the mixture stand at room temperature in a quiet corner of the kitchen overnight.

2. The next day, about 2 hours before you want to sit down for the meal, combine all the remaining dough ingredients, except the salt, in the bowl of a stand mixer. Using the dough hook attachment, mix on low for 2 minutes, until just combined. Allow the dough to rest for 10 minutes.

3. Add the salt and knead for 8 to 9 minutes on medium speed, until the dough comes cleanly away from the sides of the bowl.

4. Place the dough into a lightly oiled 4-quart (3.8 L) container and allow it to rise for 30 minutes.

5. Fold the dough by lifting one side into the middle, then repeating with the other side, sort of like folding a letter. Allow it to rise for another 30 minutes.

6. Scrape the dough out onto a floured work surface and divide it into 12 equal pieces. Shape these into balls and allow them to proof for 15 minutes (the dough will rise a little).

7. Preheat a large, well-seasoned, cast-iron skillet over medium heat.

8. Punch the balls of dough down one at a time using your fingers. Press each one out and stretch the dough by tossing it back and forth from side to side until it is fairly thin. Use a rolling pin to help if necessary.

9. Lay one of the pieces of naan dough in the hot, dry skillet and cook until it begins to blister, about 30 seconds, then flip. Repeat with the remaining pieces.

10. Brush the naan with flavored oils, herbs, or toasted spices, if desired.

The pre-ferment is a part of the dough that is mixed way ahead of time and allowed to slowly ferment to activate the yeast. Doing this creates a much more intense flavor for your breads, as well as a better texture.

table bread

MAKES 1 LARGE LOAF

One of my favorite things about Alex, besides his pizza and his handsome face, is that on any given day of the week he might decide to make a few loaves of bread. Freshly baked bread—the smell of it, the taste of it, the idea of it—every part is a great addition to our lives. I've watched him work on his techniques and bread varieties through the years, and it's been a wonderful, tasty treat for me. This recipe is not only delightful to eat, it's also a very approachable bread, as it doesn't take days to make or have too many steps involved. You will notice, though, that I've listed any metric measurements first; I highly recommend using those to ensure the best possible results, since that's what Alex uses when he makes this.

PRE-FERMENT*

480 g (3¾ cups + 1 tablespoon)
  unbleached, unbromated
  flour (preferably organic)

330 ml (⅖ cup) water

⅛ teaspoon instant yeast

DOUGH

Pre-ferment

120 g (scant 1 cup)
  unbleached, unbromated
  flour (preferably organic)

123 ml (½ cup) water

1.5 g (½ teaspoon) instant
  yeast

11 g (2 teaspoons) sea salt

1. In a large bowl, use a wooden spoon to combine all the pre-ferment ingredients together until a rough dough forms. Make sure all the flour is incorporated, then set aside to rest for 10 to 12 hours.

2. When the pre-ferment is ready, combine it with all the other dough ingredients, except the salt, in the bowl of a stand mixer. Using the dough attachment, mix on the lowest speed until a wet dough comes together, 1 to 2 minutes.

3. Allow the dough to rest for 20 minutes. (It will not rise at this stage.)

4. Turn the mixer up to the next speed (I use the 2 setting on my KitchenAid mixer) and knead the dough for 3 minutes. Add the salt and knead for another minute.

5. Using a rubber or silicone spatula, move the dough from the mixing bowl into a large bowl.

Recipe continues...

6. With wet hands, fold the dough in the way you would fold a letter to fit in an envelope—lift one side up and over toward the center, give it a good stretch, and then repeat with the other side. Leave the dough to ferment for 3 hours to develop the flavor and the gluten. Give the dough another fold every hour.

7. After the dough has risen substantially, scrape it out of the bowl onto a lightly floured work surface. I like to use a little rubber scraper tool to work with the dough at this point, but a blunt knife or even a piece of hard cardboard will do. Scrape under the dough to make sure it's loose from the sides. The dough will be very sticky.

8. Holding the scraper in one hand and cupping the dough with the other, push the dough onto itself to create a rounded mound. Allow it to rest for 10 minutes, then flip the dough over so the top is now the bottom.

9. To shape the loaf, start from the top of the dough and fold it toward the center, then fold from the left to the center, then from the right to the center. Repeat this step, working your way vertically down the dough to tuck it all up. When you get to the end, fold the top end over to meet the bottom end and pinch it lightly. Now you should have a taller, more upright ball. Place a hand on each side of the dough and roll them a bit to stretch the dough taut.

10. Cover a basket, bowl, or colander with a floured kitchen towel and place the shaped dough seam side up (so that the stretched top of the dough faces downward) in the bowl to proof for 2½ hours before baking. It should double in size at this point in the process.

11. Right before you're ready to bake the bread, heat a cast-iron Dutch oven to 450°F (230°C).

12. Turn the dough out of the container and into the heated Dutch oven. Lightly score the top with a knife, then cover and bake for 30 minutes. Remove the lid and bake another 20 minutes.

13. Remove the baked bread from the pot and allow it to cool for at least 1 hour before digging in.

MONEY-SAVING TIP: Although it may be a bit time-consuming to make, homemade bread is a great money-saving trick. Bake multiple batches of bread at a time and keep the extras in the freezer; you can freeze whole loaves or pre-slice them if you prefer. To defrost an entire loaf of bread, heat the oven to 250°F (120°C), wrap the loaf in aluminum foil, and pop it into the oven for 15 to 20 minutes. Allow it to cool a bit before unwrapping, then enjoy! Did you pre-slice your bread? Simply pull a piece out of the freezer and pop it right into the oven or toaster.

A NOTE FROM ALEX

This recipe is designed to bring delicious, bakery-quality bread into your home without too much work. The schedule is flexible enough that you can time it to have fresh bread for breakfast or for dinner—see the suggested schedules below for a guide to when to complete each stage. The amount of time needed for some of the steps may seem long, but they're really very passive. The active work of mixing, kneading, and shaping the bread takes just minutes; the real work occurs during the fermentation process while you're sleeping or at work. Just try it and see for yourself!

REAL-TIME SCHEDULE TO HAVE FRESH BREAD FOR DINNER:

The night before: Mix the pre-ferment and allow it to rest overnight.

The next morning: Mix the dough. Allow it to ferment (20 minutes), then shape it, and set the dough out to proof (2½ hours).

That afternoon: Bake the dough.

That evening: Fresh bread for dinner!

REAL-TIME SCHEDULE TO HAVE FRESH BREAD FOR BREAKFAST:

The morning before: Mix the pre-ferment and allow it to rest during the day.

Early that evening: Mix the dough. Allow it to ferment (20 minutes), then shape it, and set the dough out to proof (2½ hours).

Later that evening: Cover the risen dough with a towel and place it in the refrigerator overnight.

Early the next day: Bake the dough first thing in the morning.

After waking up the family: Fresh bread for breakfast!

plantain corn bread

SERVES 4 AS A DINNER ACCOMPANIMENT

You may be surprised to hear that corn and plantains go beautifully together, but they absolutely do. All you need is an overripe plantain to make some really, really good corn bread. Plus, when you add plantain, there's no need for eggs, egg replacer, applesauce (or banana). I know you'll be impressed by this simple but savvy creation.

1 super-ripe plantain (black is good!)

1 cup (250 ml) almond or soy milk

4 tablespoons dairy-free butter, melted, or canola oil

1 cup (125 g) all-purpose flour

1 cup (140 g) cornmeal

¼ cup (57 g) sugar

¾ teaspoon salt

1 tablespoon + ¼ teaspoon baking soda

1. Preheat the oven to 425°F (220°C).

2. Peel the plantain and puree it with the milk and butter in a medium bowl.

3. Combine the flour, cornmeal, sugar, salt, and baking soda in a large bowl.

4. Fold the plantain mixture into the dry ingredients.

5. Once the batter is fully combined, pour it into a 9-inch (23 cm) cast-iron skillet and bake for 20 to 25 minutes, until golden.

A NOTE ABOUT THIS RECIPE

One of the most common vegan egg substitutes is banana, which is fantastic for banana-lovers—but some of us actually loathe bananas. Even now, as I write this, my nose crinkles as I think about bananas. I just can't. However, despite my complete dislike of bananas, I adore its close relative, the plantain. So one day, I'm in the kitchen making chili, and in front of me sits this sad, lonely plantain. It was just begging to be used. I thought to myself (and to it), "You may be my delicious solution to so many problems." Then I blended it up, tried it out in place of eggs in some corn bread, and— *blammo*—magic! I had solved my big banana-hating problem, saved a plantain from going to waste, and created something simply delicious in the process.

basic tortillas

Although we don't always make our own tortillas, we do it pretty often. And we always try to prepare them ourselves when guests come over—it just helps the meal feel more special and extra home-cooked. Really, though, making them yourself doesn't take very long or require much effort, and it costs mere pennies. I try to always keep a bag of masa on hand, since it lasts a while and allows you to create taco night whenever you want without having to run out to the store for more tortillas. Handmade tortillas aren't something I grew up with, but I'm happy it's something we've added to our family tradition.

¾ cup (175 ml) warm water

Pinch of salt

1 cup (115 g) masa flour

1. In a medium bowl, mix together the water and the salt until the salt dissolves.

2. Add the masa and combine until a ball of dough forms.

3. Roll the dough into golf ball–size spheres.

4. Preheat a griddle over medium heat.

5. Press the balls flat using either a tortilla press or a heavy pan. Use parchment paper to prevent the dough from sticking to the surface.

6. Cook each tortilla on the griddle until steam rises, about 30 seconds. Flip over and repeat.

7. Wrap the tortillas in a kitchen towel to keep them warm until you're ready to serve them. Make these for the Really Good Vegetable Tacos (page 174) or Black Beans (page 176), or any other dish you like!

TIP FOR LEFTOVERS: Use any tortillas that don't get eaten in the Corn & Potato Chowder (page 128).

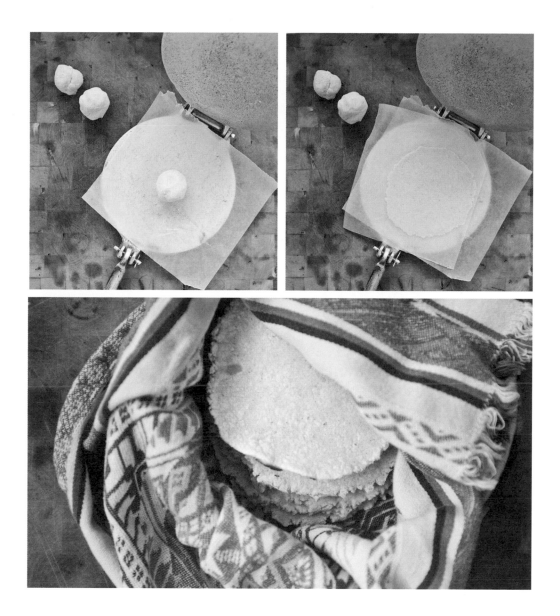

KID-FRIENDLY TIP: While a tortilla press isn't necessary to make these, it is a beautiful-looking item for a kitchen—and more than that, it's a fun tool for children to use and a good way for them to be involved in the process.

biscuits

I didn't grow up eating biscuits, and I couldn't even tell you the first time I had one. But I can tell you that these particular ones are simply wonderful, especially when you make them with people you love and cut them into heart shapes. Serve them with mushroom gravy for a filling meal (see the Biscuits with Mushroom Gravy, page 32), or with butter and/or your favorite jam for an unfussy breakfast. Or knead in a handful of your favorite chopped herbs, as called for in the White Bean Stew with Herbed Biscuits on page 142.

2 cups (250 g) all-purpose flour

2 tablespoons baking powder

½ teaspoon salt

4 tablespoons dairy-free butter

¾ cup (175 ml) almond or soy milk

1. Preheat the oven to 450°F (230°C).

2. Combine the flour, baking powder, and salt in a large bowl.

3. Add the butter in individual clumps. Use your hands to break up the butter and completely blend it into the flour mixture.

4. Pour in the milk and mix until a ball of dough forms.

5. Knead the dough for 2 to 3 minutes on a floured surface.

6. Roll the dough out using a rolling pin and cut it into circles (or hearts!) using a biscuit- or cookie-cutter, or you can just pull apart golf ball–size pieces of the dough and form them into balls.

7. Place the biscuits on an ungreased baking sheet and bake for 9 to 12 minutes, until plump and lightly toasted. The exact time will depend on the size of your biscuits.

8. Enjoy them warm out of the oven, or munch on them later!

piecrust

Oh, piecrust—you are the vessel for everything that is good and delicious in this world. I use a dairy-free butter in my recipe, since it adds a wonderfully rich flavor, but it's possible to make this with vegetable shortening as well. This is the crust I use for my Chickpea Pot Pie (page 140) and my Sweet Potato Pie (page 282). One last note: make sure you put a lot of love into this piecrust—that always makes everything better!

2½ cups (312 g) all-purpose flour

1 tablespoon sugar

2 sticks (1 cup [230 g]) very cold dairy-free butter

½ cup (125 ml) ice cold water

1. Combine the flour and sugar in a large bowl.

2. Slice the cold butter into small pieces and add it to the flour and sugar mixture.

3. Using a pastry blender, a food processor, or your hands, mix in the butter. I use my hands, since it's a pretty easy cleanup. The flour will clump together with the butter. Once you have itty-bitty clumps, you're good to go!

4. Pour about ¼ cup (60 ml) of the ice cold water over the flour and butter and begin to work it in around the edges of the dough with your hands. If necessary, add the remaining water a tiny bit at a time, kneading the dough with your hands, until a solid ball forms. I typically don't use more than ½ cup (125 ml) total. Just be sure to add the water slowly—you don't want a mushy ball, but you don't want it too dry, either.

5. Pat the ball of dough smooth, wrap it in plastic wrap, and place it in the fridge to rest for at least an hour, or overnight if you're planning on making pie the next day.

6. Bake it as the recipe directs, and enjoy crispy, flaky goodness!

sweet
treats

chocolate chip cookies

I n my opinion, chocolate chip cookies are the only kind of cookies worth eating. Don't give me peanut butter or oatmeal—just chocolate chips. Nothing else matters. Please note, though, that it's never a good idea to talk about cookies when you don't actually have cookies or the ingredients to make them in your home. Imagine the horror scene: it's very late at night, your mouth is watering for cookies, and the store is closed. Only discuss cookies during hours that the supermarket is open! Consider yourself warned.

2¼ cups (281 g) all-purpose flour

½ teaspoon salt

1 teaspoon baking soda

¾ cup (170 g) sugar

¾ cup (150 g) brown sugar

1 cup (230 g) dairy-free butter

1 "egg" using 1½ to 2 teaspoons ener-G egg replacer combined with 2½ tablespoons water, or your other favorite egg replacer*

1 teaspoon vanilla extract

One 8- to 10-ounce (226 to 263 g) bag vegan chocolate chips (amount depends on how chocolatey you want your cookies to be!)

1. Move a rack to the middle of the oven. Preheat the oven to 375°F (190°C).

2. Mix together the flour, salt, and baking soda in a medium bowl. Set aside.

3. In a large bowl, mix together the sugar, brown sugar, and butter, until the butter is well combined.

4. Mix the "egg" and the vanilla into the sugar and butter mixture.

5. Add the dry ingredients to the wet ingredients, a little bit at a time, until everything is mixed in.

6. Stir in the chocolate chips. You can add as many or as few as you'd like—I usually end up using about three-quarters of the bag.

7. Rolling a little bit of the dough in your hand, create small 1½-inch (4 cm) balls. Place each ball on an ungreased cookie sheet, about 2 inches (5 cm) apart.

8. Bake on the middle oven rack for 7 to 9 minutes. The timing will vary depending on the size of your cookies.

Recipe continues...

A NOTE ABOUT THIS RECIPE

I'll admit right off the bat that I don't expect to win any health awards for my desserts, since I'm not a big fan of subbing out ingredients just to make it "low-fat" or "low-sugar." If things happen to be low-fat or low-sugar? All the better! It turns out, however, that there's no real way to make a truly delicious cookie that's missing fat and sugar. You might be able to get a decent-tasting one, but a really good cookie that's worth drooling about later? Nope. I've had plenty of healthy desserts that are absolutely delicious—such as raw fruit pies and frozen extruded fruits, but you won't find those recipes here. The desserts I've included in this section are rich enough to fulfill all your sweet-treat cravings.

9. When the cookies are golden, remove the sheet from the oven and allow the cookies to cool.

10. Pop a still-warm one into your mouth and savor the chocolatey goodness!

I use a store-bought egg-replacer in this recipe, but you can probably substitute a Flax Egg (page 35) instead, although I haven't tried that myself. I don't recommend using bananas or applesauce or anything like that; the cookies just won't be the same.

TIP FOR LEFTOVERS: Hahahaha! Seriously, it's hard to resist cookies. One thing that can help your batch last longer is to leave a portion out to snack on for the next few days and store the rest in the freezer. When you're ready to eat them later, simply pull them out to defrost on the counter. It can be a slow and painful wait, though, so you can always warm one up in the oven and eat it with ice cream while you wait for the rest to thaw.

chocolate chip coffee brownies

MAKES 12 BROWNIES

These brownies are perfection. You will instantly fall in love and have a hard time saying no to snacking on them. The coffee provides a subtly rich flavor that's not overpowering, with just the right amount of kick. Avoiding caffeine? No worries; you can substitute water (but coffee is better).

1. Move a rack to the middle of the oven. Preheat the oven to 350°F (175°C).

2. Combine the flour, sugar, cocoa powder, baking powder, and salt in a large mixing bowl.

3. Add the coffee or espresso and the vanilla; mix until combined. Slowly mix in the melted butter. When the mixture is nice and smooth, fold in the chocolate chips.

4. Pour the mixture into a buttered and floured 9 x 13-inch (23 x 33 cm) baking pan and bake on the middle oven rack for 40 to 45 minutes, until a toothpick inserted into the center comes out clean. Let cool before serving.

2½ cups (312 g) all-purpose flour

2 cups (450 g) sugar

¾ cup (66 g) cocoa powder

1¼ teaspoons baking powder

1½ teaspoons salt

1 cup (250 ml) strong coffee or espresso

1 teaspoon vanilla extract

1½ cups (340 g) dairy-free butter, melted

2 handfuls of vegan chocolate chips

s'mores bars

My roommate in college got me hooked on a variation of this dessert that was loaded with butter, sugar, chocolate, and all the best headache-inducing ingredients in life. Since my family tends to steer clear of extra sugar, I don't make this dish often, but it's a really good one if you're looking for a something indulgent or a great treat to bring to a kiddo's birthday party.

½ cup (110 g) brown rice syrup

1 teaspoon agar agar

2 tablespoons confectioners' sugar

5 cups (187 g) graham cracker cereal (there are a few vegan brands out there; we typically grab a box of Cascadian Farm Graham Crunch)

2 cups (440 g) dairy-free dark chocolate chips

1. Line a shallow 9 x 9-inch (23 x 23 cm) baking dish with parchment paper.

2. Combine the rice syrup, agar agar, and confectioners' sugar in a small saucepan. Place the saucepan over low heat and stir continuously while the mixture slowly heats.

3. Pour the cereal into a large bowl.

4. When the mixture on the stove is well combined, pour it over the cereal and mix everything well, being careful not to break the cereal or burn your hands!

5. Stir in the chocolate chips.

6. Spread the mixture evenly across the lined baking dish, to at least 1-inch (2.5 cm) thickness. Don't worry if it doesn't cover the entire bottom of the pan.

7. Place the dish in the fridge and allow it to cool completely, about 2 hours.

8. Once it's cooled, remove the dish from the fridge, tear away the parchment paper, and cut into 2-inch (5 cm) squares.

9. Eat and enjoy!

TIP FOR LEFTOVERS: Store any remaining cereal bars in fridge for up to 5 days or in the freezer for up to a month.

warm berry galettes

These little tarts are slightly more challenging than a pie to make, but they look impressive when they're done. Especially beautiful for summer parties, they really work perfectly for any occasion. Use a large cup or bowl as a stencil for perfectly cut dough.

1. To make the dough, mix together the flour, 2 tablespoons of sugar, salt, and lemon zest in a large bowl. Add the shortening and use a mixer or pastry cutter to incorporate it into the dry ingredients, until the mixture looks crumbly. Slowly add the water while mixing the dough with your hands or a mixer, until a ball forms.

2. Wrap the ball in parchment paper and refrigerate for at least 30 minutes, until ready to use.

3. To make the filling, slice or chop the strawberries and place them in a large bowl. Add the remaining sugar, lemon juice, vanilla, salt and toss. Refrigerate until needed.

4. Preheat the oven to 375°F (190°C).

5. To create the galette, remove the dough from the fridge and place it on a lightly floured work surface. Roll the dough out to ¼-inch (6 mm) thickness. Cut the dough into four 6-inch (15 cm) circles. Place the dough on a baking sheet lined with parchment paper.

6. Place a quarter of the strawberry filling in the center of each disk, leaving a 1-inch (2.5 cm) perimeter around the edge. Gently fold up and crimp the edges of the tart crust over the filling. Be sure to close any cracks or holes around the edge. Brush the crust with the honey and water mixture.

7. Bake for 30 to 40 minutes, until lightly golden brown. Serve warm.

2⅓ cups (292 g) all-purpose flour

4 heaping tablespoons granulated sugar, divided

1 teaspoon salt

Zest and juice of 1 lemon

⅔ cup (150 g) vegetable shortening

2 to 3 tablespoons water

2 pounds (450 g, or scant 1½ pints) strawberries

1 teaspoon vanilla extract

Pinch of salt

A few tablespoons of honey thinned with a splash of water (the ratio will vary, depending on your type of honey, but you want to create a spreadable mixture for coating the crust)

rice pudding

This recipe for a favorite dish from my childhood isn't quite the same as the ones I grew up with, since those versions were packed with dairy. I substitute almond milk for traditional milk and use coconut milk in place of the condensed milk that's commonly found in Latin American variations. I sweeten the pudding with honey, but you can easily use traditional sugar if you prefer. Either way, I suggest adding an extra helping of love—my mother and grandmothers served it this way, and I guarantee it makes the pudding taste extra-special.

2 tablespoons coconut oil

1 cup (185 g) uncooked white rice

2 cinnamon sticks

½ teaspoon ground cinnamon

1? cups (350 ml) water

3 cups (700 ml) almond milk (or other dairy-free milk of choice)

One 14-ounce (400 ml) can coconut milk

½ cup (113 g) honey or brown rice syrup

1. Heat the coconut oil in a large heavy-bottomed pan over medium heat. Add the rice and stir, coating the rice with oil and allowing it to lightly toast. Mix in the cinnamon sticks and ground cinnamon.

2. Stir in the water, then bring the mixture to a boil. Lower the heat to a simmer and cook, uncovered, for 10 minutes, stirring occasionally.

3. Add the almond milk and bring the mixture to a boil before lowering the heat back to a simmer. Cook for 15 minutes, stirring occasionally.

4. Stir in the coconut milk and honey or brown rice syrup. Simmer for about 15 minutes. You want the rice to be well cooked, but you should be aware that the rice pudding will thicken slightly as it cools. Feel free to add a splash more almond milk for a thinner consistency, or you can cook it longer for an even thicker texture—it all depends on your preference.

5. Serve hot, warm, or even cold with a sprinkle of cinnamon and/or sugar on top.

TIP: After this pudding has been refrigerated for a while, it can become quite dense since the coconut milk hardens as it cools. Reheating the rice pudding back to a slightly warmer temperature will loosen it up again. If you reheat it on the stovetop, add a touch more milk if necessary to restore some moisture.

A NOTE ABOUT THIS RECIPE

This dish is also known as *arroz con leche* if you're my Colombian maternal grandmother or *riz au lait* if you're my French-Canadian paternal grandmother. "Rice pudding" in any language always makes me think of these amazing women. Actually, while we're on the topic of amazing women and rice pudding, it makes me think of my mom, too. It was the only "real dessert" my mother would make while I was growing up. She would serve it hot, while my paternal grandmother would serve it cold. To this day, I can't decide which way I prefer—I like the flavor best when it's cold, but I find comfort in it served warm.

healthy and delicious!

orange-infused coconut whipped cream

MAKES ABOUT 1 CUP (120 G)

Whipped cream was one of my favorite treats growing up. I ate it on everything. Waffles weren't complete unless they had a heaping dollop of the stuff on top. Though I no longer require whipped cream with my meals, man, this recipe really is the icing on the cake—the whipped cream on my waffle, if you will. This is absolutely perfect on Garam Masala Pancakes (page 34), Tropical Waffles (page 36), and so many other dishes. The most important thing to remember when making this is to refrigerate the coconut milk overnight (or longer), or else the recipe won't work.

1. Carefully open the can of refrigerated coconut milk without shaking it. Scoop out the top layer of coconut cream, being careful not to get any of the liquid from the bottom (see the Tip below for suggestions on using this leftover coconut water). Place the coconut cream in a cold, large, metal mixing bowl.

2. Add the remaining ingredients and beat with a handheld or stand mixer for about 5 minutes, until the cream is whipped and fluffy. Yum!

3. Serve on waffles, pancakes, ice cream, fruit—anything and everything.

One 14-ounce (400 ml) can full-fat coconut milk, refrigerated overnight

1 tablespoon sugar or sweetener substitute

Zest of 2 oranges

1 tablespoon orange juice

TIP: Don't toss out the coconut water. You can use it in smoothies, such as the Mango Smoothie (page 290), or even in cocktails!

sweet potato pie

I created this pie for my extended family, who are intense in their quest for all-things-sweet-potato. Mashed, fried, grilled, baked—you name it, and they'll devour it. I've put my own spin on a sweet potato pie by making it with coconut fat, which adds a smooth richness that's almost magical. Although I'm generally not a big fan of sweet potatoes (both Marlowe and I will happily eat a creamy sweet potato soup, but we pass on sweet potato fries), the addition of coconut milk to this recipe made me fall in love with sweet potato pie. It's wonderful paired with vanilla bean ice cream, so be sure to try it that way, too!

One 14-ounce (400 ml) can full-fat coconut milk, refrigerated overnight

⅓ cup (104 ml) maple syrup

2 tablespoons arrowroot powder

2½ cups (500 g, or about 2 medium) cooked, peeled, and pureed sweet potato*

½ cup (113 g) sugar

2 teaspoons vanilla extract

Cinnamon for sprinkling on top (optional)

Piecrust (page 268), refrigerated until ready for use

1. Carefully, without shaking it, open the can of refrigerated coconut milk, scoop out the fat (the thick white cream that sits on top), and place it into a food processor. Keep the liquid that's left over in the can—you'll use it later.

2. Add the maple syrup and arrowroot and blend until completely smooth.

3. Add the sweet potato, sugar, and vanilla and puree, mixing in coconut water as needed. You want the filling to be a thick, very smooth, almost paste-like cream.

4. Preheat the oven to 350°F (175°C).

5. Pull the refrigerated dough from the fridge and place it on a floured surface. Roll the dough out into a 12-inch (30 cm) circle. It doesn't have to be perfectly round; just make sure it's large enough to fit your pie dish. Carefully press the rolled-out crust into the dish and cut off the extra dough around the edges using scissors or a sharp knife.

6. Scoop the filling into the pie pan.

Recipe continues...

You can bake or boil the sweet pota-toes—I wrap mine in aluminum foil and bake them at 450°F (230°C) for 1 hour, then peel off the skin after they cool down a bit.

7. If you prefer a two-crust pie, you can take the extra dough and re-roll it out to make shapes or a lattice for the top. Sprinkle the top with cinnamon, if using.

8. Bake the pie until the crust begins to brown. This could be anywhere from 40 to 60 minutes, depending on your oven. Once the crust is golden brown, remove the pie from the oven and allow it to cool completely.

9. Serve at room temperature, or sometimes slightly chilled is preferable. Refrigerate any leftovers.

smoothies

chocolate smoothie

This is hands-down our favorite smoothie. It's incredibly tasty, plus it's packed with protein, fiber, and tons of other good stuff.

¼ Hass avocado

1 to 1¼ cups (250 to 300 ml) almond milk (or other dairy-free milk of choice)

2 squares of raw cacao goji bars (you can find these 1-inch [2.5 cm] cubes in the bulk bin of many health food stores, or easily order them online with a quick online search)

4 Medjool dates, pitted

1. Place all the ingredients in a blender and puree until very smooth.

2. Enjoy the chocolatey goodness.

ADULT-FRIENDLY TIP: I sometimes add a shot of espresso to this recipe, and it's freaking amazing.

strawberry oat smoothie

This smoothie is such a treat. My mom made a similar version while I was growing up in her effort to get us kids to eat better, but I've changed the recipe a bit here by adding dates and oatmeal for an extra dose of good health. I find it rather ironic that now, within my own family, we enjoy this as a special treat, whereas my mother fed it to me for nutrition when I was a child. Although healthy eating habits may take time to develop, this should be a hit "dessert" with even the pickiest kids.

Combine all the ingredients in a blender and puree until "smoothie." Take a sip and think to yourself, "Whoa . . . this tastes awesome!"

KID-FRIENDLY TIP: You can try sneaking a handful of spinach into this one, if you'd like.

¼ cup (25 g) quick oats

1 cup (250 ml) vanilla almond milk

4 Medjool dates, pitted

¾ cup (165 g) whole frozen strawberries

THE PLANTIFUL TABLE

avocado smoothie

You're probably more familiar with the ubiquitous Hass avocado, but Florida avocados can be a nice change of pace. If you can find Florida avocados at a farmers' market or, better yet, pluck them directly from a friend's yard, they're simply incredible. Unfortunately, the Florida avocados purchased at the supermarket have a tendency to be really watery and not so appetizing. Don't worry if you don't have easy access to fresh, delicious Florida avocados—I call for a Hass in this recipe, so it works for everyone. If you do have a Florida avocado on hand, though, adjust the recipe according to the size of your giant fruit.

1. Blend the avocado, milk, and sweetener until completely smooth, adding additional milk if necessary to reach your desired consistency.

2. Place the boba into a large cup and pour the smoothie on top.

3. Enjoy!

½ Hass avocado

¾ to 1 cup (175 to 250 ml) dairy-free milk

3 tablespoons honey or agave syrup

¼ cup (45 g) boba (tapioca pearls), prepared and chilled

mango smoothie

Drinking this smoothie will instantly make you feel like you're in the tropics!

1 cup (100 g) chopped mango

½ cup (125 ml) coconut milk

Juice of 1 lime (about 1½ to 2 tablespoons)

½ cup (125 g) ice

Pinch of salt

Blend all the ingredients together in a blender until smooth. Drink and feel refreshed!

ADULT-FRIENDLY TIP: If you want to be a little wild, you could try this spiked with a bit of booze, too!

vanilla nut protein smoothie

MAKES 1 LARGE SMOOTHIE

During my pregnancy, I made a variation of this smoothie every single day, with added chocolate protein powder. The nuts add a ton of protein, while the raisins add a nice boost of fiber. The vanilla bean, though—that's the true star of the recipe.

¼ cup (30 g) raw cashews

¼ cup (35 g) raw almonds (slivers or whole)

¼ cup (40 g) raisins

About ⅓ of a vanilla bean—I'll leave the exact amount up to you, but a third of a pod should be enough

1 cup (250 ml) dairy-free milk

1. If you can plan ahead, soak all the ingredients in water overnight before blending.

2. Combine all the ingredients in a high-speed blender and blend until completely smooth. It will require more blend time if you haven't soaked everything beforehand.

3. Serve this smoothie very cold.

TIP: Not sure how to work with a fresh vanilla bean? Carefully make a slit down the side, open up the pod, and scrape the insides into your recipe.

for your dog

homemade dog food

Although we don't currently feed our dogs, Jerry and Waylon, a vegan diet, at one point, before I got pregnant and had a baby (now kid) to raise, I spoiled my first dog, Jerry, in every possible way, including making him special doggy food. I once read that the oldest living dog on record was fed a diet of rice, lentils, and vegetables. Judging by my dog's skin and appearance when he ate that way, I completely believe it. If you have the time and interest to cook homemade meals for your dog, here's a super-simple recipe to use. You'll notice in a week or so how soft and shiny your pup's coat is.

½ cup (93 g) brown rice

⅓ cup (65 g) dried lentils

1½ cups (350 ml) water

½ cup (70 g) diced mixed vegetables—no onions or garlic!

Combine all the ingredients in a small saucepan and bring to a boil over medium-high heat. Cover and simmer for 45 minutes, until the rice is fully cooked. Allow it to cool a bit before serving it to your dog.

TIP: You can use the scraps from making Vegetable Stock (page 116) in your dog food mix, but please pick out the onions since they're extremely toxic to dogs. Other items you should never feed your puppy? Avocados, caffeine, alcohol, chocolate, grapes, raisins, macadamia nuts, peaches, persimmons, plums, salt, or any foods sweetened with xylitol.

Note: If you feed your dogs beets, don't be alarmed when their poop is red!

peanut butter dog biscuits

We've learned that while our dogs may not always eat a vegan diet, they don't do well with meaty doggy treats. This recipe is a quick and easy plant-based snack for your pups to enjoy. Feel free to get creative with the cookie-cutter shape!

½ cup (125 ml) almond milk

½ cup (150 g) peanut butter

1 Flax Egg (page 35)

1 cup (125 g) whole wheat flour

1. Preheat the oven to 400°F (200°C).

2. In a medium bowl, combine the milk and peanut butter until smooth.

3. Add the Flax Egg and mix until combined.

4. Pour the flour into a large bowl. Gradually stir the peanut butter mixture into the flour until a dough forms.

5. Knead the dough by hand for a few minutes, then roll it out on a floured surface to about ½-inch (1 cm) thick.

6. Cut out the treats using cookie cutters or a knife.

7. Place the treats on a foil-covered baking sheet and bake 8 to 10 minutes, until slightly golden.

8. Allow them to cool before feeding to your dog or storing in an airtight container for later.

TIP: This recipe makes rather soft biscuits. If you'd like them to be on the crunchier side, roll them out more thinly and bake them a tad bit longer. I find the dogs make less of a mess eating them when they're chewy, though, so take that into consideration. You can also make these thicker if you want, but they'll require a longer baking time—just check them every few minutes until they're done.

acknowledgments

Thanks to the help of so many people (and a tiny bit of my own skillful stubbornness), this long-time goal and amazing project is now completed, which calls for an endless number of "hoorays!" and "thank-yous!"

To my amazing husband, Alex, for sharing a love of food, for making me pizza, and for being my other half in this delicious life. Thank you for being the steady, super-tidy, bull-headed rock that I very much need. For not only lifting my spirits, but also for being by my side and a part of the process on so many days. Without you, there would be far less bread, noodles, and sambal. Thank you for your help. I'm grateful to share so many meals with you and your handsome face.

To my daughter, the inspiration for so many things in my life. My little sidekick. My lover of green foods. My reason for spending more time in the kitchen. Miss Marlowe Paloma, you've changed my life for the better. Thanks for helping me make this cookbook and for constantly asking, "Why is your cookbook not done yet?" I'll cook for you for as long as you let me.

To my mother, for always going above and beyond for me. For teaching me refinement. I'm sorry I didn't like your green soup. Thank you for making me eat it anyway.

For my dad, for gifting me the gift of dry humor, bad jokes, sarcasm, and picky eating habits. This book and my world would be far more boring without those.

To all my family and friends, for always believing in me, supporting me, trying my food (even the failed recipes), and cheering me on. Thanks for not giving up on our friendship every time I hermit-ed myself away into work mode. I'm grateful to share my meals (and wine) with you.

To Ani Chamichian, for seeing my work and my vision and for believing in my ability to create this book. And to Sasha Tropp, Matthew Lore, and the rest of The Experiment team for taking a chance on me. For the countless correspondence back and forth, for guiding me, and for allowing me to be myself. This wouldn't have happened without all of you.

To Hannah Mayo, thank you for giving me your time, patience, and talent to capture such beautiful pictures of my family. I'm glad to not only call you a photographer but now, also, a friend. (hannahmayophotography.com)

To my blog readers, thank you for coming back to the *ohdeardrea* blog time and time again. Thank you for not only being inspired by my meals and my stories, but for inspiring my life, as well. It's been an amazing experience to connect with so many of you in so many ways. Thank you for your endless amount of support through everything delicious and real in my life.

And many thanks to Anthropologie, Dot & Army, and all my friends who helped add to my kitchen dish- and serving-ware collection. Thank you for adding those extra little touches of sparkle.

Really, an endless number of thank-yous to everyone. I can't imagine my world without the tremendous amount of goodness you all have brought. Thank you for letting me be a part of your lives. I am forever grateful. I hope to give a million hugs, thank-yous, and cookies to all of you one day.

resources

Glossary

AGAR AGAR: A vegetarian substitute for gelatin

BRAGG'S LIQUID AMINOS: Similar to soy sauce, but containing extra healthy amino acids

ARROWROOT POWDER: An easily digestible starch, great for use as a thickener in sauces or in place of eggs

BÁHN MÌ: Vietnamese for "bread/baguette"; frequently used as a term for a meat-filled sandwich; Báhn Mì Chay (page 74) is the vegetarian version

BLACK RICE: A super-grain packed with iron, vitamin E, and antioxidants; a healthy rice option

BOBA (TAPIOCA PEARLS): Tiny dime-size balls made from tapioca; typically served as a fun, chewy addition to drinks

BONIATO: A variety of sweet potato originally cultivated in Colombia and Peru

CACAO NIBS: Roasted, crushed, cocoa-bean pieces

COCONUT MILK YOGURT: Yogurt made from coconut milk rather than animal milk; it's good to mention that all coconut (or soy) yogurts are not necessarily dairy-free—be sure to check the labels!

DAIKON RADISH: A large, mild-flavored radish that basically looks like a giant, fat, white carrot; found in many Asian dishes

DRIED COCONUT PALM SUGAR: A sugar derived from coconut-palm nectar; it's still a sugar and still not great for your health, but it's slightly better for you than cane sugar!

DRIED KOMBU: Dried edible kelp that's harvested in Japan and Korea; high in nutrients such as calcium and iron, and wonderful in Asian broths

GARAM MASALA: A delicious Indian seasoning blend; somewhat similar to cinnamon, except less spicy and more sweet

GOCHUJANG (FERMENTED RED CHILI PASTE): A fermented Korean condiment made from red chiles, glutinous rice, and soybeans

GROUND ACHIOTE (GROUND ANNATTO): A natural coloring and flavoring agent from the achiote tree; red in color, slightly nutty, peppery, and sweet

KIMCHI: A fermented Korean side dish typically made from cabbage, radish, scallion, or cucumber; a great addition to many meals, since it's both incredibly healthy for you and delicious

KOREAN CHILI POWDER: A spicy chili powder found in Asian markets; you can substitute this for a spicy Indian chili powder, but it's different than the usual American chili-powder option—it's a whole lot spicier!

LIQUID SMOKE: Made from smoke created out of wood chips and water; a wonderful flavoring agent to add smokiness to any meal, it can be found at most grocery stores in the essences/extracts section

MALANGA: A tropical vegetable similar to taro root; also known as *eddoe*

MASA: Short for *masa de maíz,* this can refer to a corn flour, meal, or dough

MASAREPA: A pre-cooked corn flour used for making arepas; we typically buy Goya brand since it's the most common

MASECA TAMALE FLOUR: A fine corn flour; perfect for making tamales

MISO PASTE: A thick, salty paste made from fermented soybeans; miso can be found in a few different colors and varieties, and all taste wonderful and are really great for you—miso is high in probiotics, amino acids, and B vitamins, especially B12, making it a great pantry addition for vegans

NUTRITIONAL YEAST: A favorite topping or recipe addition for many vegans, it has a strong nutty, cheesy flavor and can be found fortified with B12; try it on popcorn—it's delicious!

PIMENTÓN: A Spanish smoked paprika made from the air-dried fruits of a chile pepper; you have a few different options: spicy (*pimentón picante*), semi-spicy (*pimentón agridulce*), or sweet (*pimentón dulce*); our absolute favorite is the sweet variety, although some of my recipes call for the spicy kind

PRE-FERMENT: A fermentation starter used in bread-making, sometimes referred to as the "mother dough"

RAW CACAO GOJI BARS: One-inch squares of healthy goodness, made primarily from raw dates, nuts, and seeds; typically found in the bulk bin section of many natural food stores, or you can search for them online

SAMBAL (CHILE PEPPER SAUCE): An Asian sauce made from an assortment of chile peppers; if you're vegan, be sure to check labels, since some varieties contain fish sauce or shrimp paste

SOBA NOODLES: A thin wheat noodle commonly used in Asian dishes

TAMARIND PUREE: Tamarind is a pod-like, sweet-and-sour fruit; I recommend buying the pre-pureed version, since it can be a difficult task to process it yourself

TAMARI: Similar to soy sauce, but containing less (or no) gluten

TARO: A starchy root vegetable related to the malanga; native to Southeast Asia, taro is eaten by cultures all over the world

TEMPEH: Fermented soybeans in a cake or patty-like form; it can be used in place of tofu, but it's much more easily digestible and has an incredibly distinct natural flavor that's sweet and nutty yet bitter

YUCA: A super-starchy root vegetable with a thick brown skin, it has a softer, silkier taste and feel than potatoes; also called cassava

Where to Shop

I know it's a cliché, but buying from your local farmer (one who practices organic standards) is your best bet for fresh produce. We typically do our non-farmers'-market shopping at Whole Foods, because it's one of the only "natural" supermarkets in our area. Our local grocer is bringing in more specialty and organic options, but these items are typically much pricier in small-scale stores. Asian markets, big and small, are a great resource for certain noodles, sauces, and hard-to-find tropical vegetables. If you can't find a specialty item near you, it's amazing what you can order online these days. Things like soy sauce, vinegar—basically anything you want—can be purchased from Amazon or other websites.

Recommendations

Books

- One of the first books I recommend to people is Mark Bittman's *How to Cook Everything Vegetarian*. It's a great place to learn the basics, such as how long to roast, boil, or sauté a specific vegetable.
- If I had to pick my favorite cookbook author, it would be either Jamie Oliver or Rick Bayless. Although neither one is vegan, both are great food inspirations.

Movies

A few food-related (primarily documentary) movies that we love in our home are:

- *Food, Inc.* (2008)
- *The Harvest* (La Cosecha) (2010)
- *King Corn* (2007)
- *Food Matters* (2008)
- *Forks Over Knives* (2011)
- *The Fruit Hunters* (2012)
- *Our Daily Bread* (2005)
- *Simply Raw* (2009)
- *Ratatouille* (2007), of course!

index

C

D

T

about the author

ANDREA DUCLOS, more commonly known as Drea, is the creator of the popular lifestyle and cooking blog *ohdeardrea* at ohdeardreablog.com. A fan of all things creative, she's got a big love for the simple pleasures in life, such as plant-based cooking, clean living, gardening, and design—and her daughter, Marlowe, and husband, Alex, of course. She resides in the tropics of South Florida with her tiny, wonderful family, where they live as simply, naturally, and happily as possible.